THE QUIET THREAT

ABOUT THE AUTHOR

Ronald L. Mendell worked as a legal investigator for thirteen years inquiring into diverse cases ranging from product liability to medical malpractice to financial investigations. He holds a B.S. degree in the Humanities from the University of the State of New York. Currently, he writes on science, technology, and investigative issues. His prior book, *How to Do Financial Asset Investigations,* 2nd edition, was released by Charles C Thomas, Publisher, Ltd. in late spring 2000. Charles C Thomas also published his book *Investigating Computer Crime: A Primer for Security Managers* in 1998. He currently works in technical support for a high-tech company in Austin, Texas.

THE QUIET THREAT

Fighting Industrial Espionage In America

By

RONALD L. MENDELL, B.S., C.L.I.

Certified Legal Investigator
Member, American Society for Industrial Security
Houston, Texas

CHARLES C THOMAS • PUBLISHER, LTD.
Springfield • Illinois • U.S.A.

Published and Distributed Throughout the World by

CHARLES C THOMAS • PUBLISHER, LTD.
2600 South First Street
Springfield, Illinois 62704

©*2003 by* CHARLES C THOMAS • PUBLISHER, LTD.

ISBN 0-398-07389-9 (hard)
ISBN 0-398-07390-2 (paper)

Library of Congress Catalog Card Number: 2002043567

With THOMAS BOOKS *careful attention is given to all details of manufacturing
and design. It is the Publisher's desire to present books that are satisfactory as to their
physical qualities and artistic possibilities and appropriate for their particular use.*
THOMAS BOOKS *will be true to those laws of quality that assure a good name
and good will.*

Printed in the United States of America
SR-R-3

Library of Congress Cataloging-in-Publication Data

Mendell, Ronald L.
  The quiet threat : fighting industrial espionage in America / by Robert L. Mendell.
     p. cm.
  Includes bibliographical references and index.
  ISBN 0-398-07389-9 (hard) -- ISBN 0-398-07390-2 (pbk.)
    1. Business intelligence--United States. 2. Trade secrets--United States. 3. Industries--
Securities measures--United States. I. Title.

HD38.7 .M456 2003
658.4'7--dc21

2002043567

PREFACE

Industrial espionage is a craft that has evolved over the centuries which remains persistent in its threat. During World War Two, organized espionage countermeasures came into American business practices. And these countermeasures met with success in a Cold War environment based upon industrialism where the prime adversary was a slow moving neo-medieval empire. The collapse of the Soviet Union ushered in two new factors. First, every nation became an adversary since competition moved from a military focus to an economic one. (Friendly competitors don't exist, whether foreign or domestic.) And second, keeping information "under wraps" became much harder. In a world where information resides more and more in electrons, secrecy resembles trying to stop a blizzard by waving a butterfly net. Berlin Walls or chain link security perimeters will not keep information contained within borders of our choosing. The Soviet Union could no longer hunker down behind the Kremlin's walls ignoring a world of the Internet, cellular telephones, and digital communications. We are in the same situation.

American security professionals cannot combat industrial (or corporate) espionage in the post-industrial information age without fully understanding its techniques. In fact, the term "industrial" may mislead; much of the spying now takes place against firms that do not manufacture a traditional industrial product, hence the alternate term "corporate espionage." But, history shows us that the techniques used today are adaptations of those developed in the sixteenth century and honed through the twentieth century. The text, accordingly, focuses on the similarity of industrial spycraft through time with examples from Anglo-American history. A primary goal of the book is giving the reader a real sense of how industrial spies are persistent and clever in circumventing defenses.

Another sense the book imparts to the security professional (or the student of security) is that industrial espionage creates paradoxes rather than straightforward, easy solutions. Rarely will the battles be set-piece confrontations with clear outcomes. Information's portability in an age of global digital networks may mean all the people who have your proprietary data can't be identified. Since copying, not stealing the original, can get the job done, thefts may go undetected for long time periods, making investigations difficult. Political dynamics within a company may aid industrial spies. And, constant change within a business often renders static, established security procedures obsolete rapidly.

The continuities in corporate and industrial espionage attacks are observation, knowledge, politics and power. Observation techniques range from aerial photography and satellite imagery to a spy jotting notes after a factory tour. Knowledge tools include patent research, induction, data analysis, and inference. Understanding the politics, the social dynamics within the modern corporation continues to be a powerful resource for the industrial spy. Exploiting jealousies and turf wars within corporate bureaucracies enables spies to penetrate inner sanctums. Power plays take several forms on the spy's stage: exercises in sexual power, in deception, or in prying secrets from a target through financial clout.

The effective twenty-first century security professional needs to be both a spy catcher and a spymaster, a collector of intelligence, an agent on the offensive, not just someone who implements countermeasures, a purely defensive strategy. So, the text examines both the defensive and offensive tactics necessary to fight industrial espionage. Living with paradox should be the theme for the security professional, and the book draws wisdom from political philosophers like Machiavelli to aid in that perspective.

However, the text strives to be more a history lesson or a discussion of security doctrine. It offers clear plans for action to deal with industrial espionage in a fluid, mobile, information-rich business environment. Creating new warriors against the quiet threat is its chief mission.

CONTENTS

THE QUIET THREAT

INTRODUCTION

PARADOX AND SECURITY

A young man in an age of well-defined conflict, my father knew why he was fighting Germans in Europe. Influenced by Churchill and Roosevelt, he understood the purpose behind the mud, shivering nights, killing men before they tried to kill him, and the strange mixture of brotherhood and loneliness that is warfare. The enemy had a clear face of unquestioned evil. And while he may have not gone to war with the zeal of a crusader, at least he understood and recognized the crusade.

Leaders such as Churchill could rally the average citizen with the threat's overwhelming reality. Protecting freedoms from tyranny motivate the otherwise comfort-seeking man or woman to make sacrifices. Roosevelt cited "Four Freedoms" to the American public: Freedom from Fear, Freedom of Speech and Expression, Freedom of Worship, and Freedom from Want.

"Freedom from Want" requires two foundations: free markets and economic strength. Economic strength in our time relies upon knowledge, intellectual capital. Threats against or attacks upon our physical infrastructure, our factories and transportation systems, historically we have responded to quite well. But the erosion of our intellectual capital can be slow and insidious without any drama, headlines, or tragedy on the nightly news.

And, unlike for my father or for his leaders, the enemy engaged in industrial espionage often lacks a clear face. No public crusade calls them into the light. For the evil behind the thievery may remain in the darkness, an obscured undercurrent, not perceived, even among corporate executives as a daily foe. This quiet threat robs us of jobs, economic resources, and the industrial strength to respond to crises both foreign and domestic.

The threat carries paradox. Traditional security thinking calls for the assessment of risks and the deployment of appropriate countermeasures. Clear, logical thinking to be sure, but threats may unfold outside of the game plan. So, a new paradigm emerges, which recognizes the limitations of countermeasures, and it embraces contradiction. We learn to think paradoxically, not everything is defendable. Security in the twenty-first century will resemble an ebb and flow.

Perhaps the hardest business problems are important but not urgent. Problems filled with urgency receive the attention and the resources. Stockholder meetings, quarterly earnings, market share issues, and profits all speak like thunderclaps. Industrial espionage remains a background whisper, a will-o'-the-wisp conjured by "security zealots." This demon of the information universe doesn't appear on management's daily radar, nor does it fray nerves until events are too late.

The first paradox of twenty-first century security totters on impossibility's slender edge. People do not recognize the threat, but they expect security to do everything, usually with sparse resources, to protect them against its consequences. Business leaders may authorize rudimentary expenditures for employee badges and a low-paid security force. But, if operational changes become necessary to fortify defenses, their hairs bristle, and the sidestepping of countermeasures or controls rears its head. And this reaction should not surprise the savvy security professional. American businesses dwell on short-term thinking, even about matters central to their core business. Why would they think differently about a security problem like industrial espionage? The riddle becomes: "When will the client worry about industrial espionage?" Unfortunately, quite often the answer remains the taunt, "When it is too late." If the barbarians are not at the gates, propelling management into action is challenging at best.

The second major paradox goes beyond business attitudes. It arises from the structure of the information commodity itself. Electronic information skirts about the Earth, extremely mobile, portable, and prone to subtle manipulation. The owner of proprietary data may have critical information stolen, but still retain physical possession of the original document or media. Copying isn't just easy; it is ridiculously easy. Treasure chests brimming with proprietary information zip out the door in a mundane briefcase. Or, the same documents dart across the globe via the Internet without a word of rancor or protest from anyone, and management won't be any wiser.

Susceptible to interception and analysis, routine business transactions and electronic messages travel about highways of wire and fiber optics or through the air in satellite and cellular transmissions. Anyone can learn our "private" communications or secrets travelling in cyberspace. Much of this traffic remains in plain text. While encryption provides some help against this hidden danger, cryptography acts to safeguard only when users follow correct procedures. Murphy's Law creeps into the business use of ciphers. Users intersperse plain text emails between encrypted messages, supplying clues to monitor the traffic. Habits are difficult to control. Sending the same message frequently, or repeatedly transmitting the same type of document, provides a cryptographer a foothold to break a cipher. Not following encryption procedures stumbles into everyday business practice. Don't expect a business to operate with the stringent information handling guidelines of the CIA or the Defense Department.

Electronic information has inherent vulnerabilities. Unlike cash or valuable commodities, locking electrons in a safe usually is not a viable option. In order to be productive for a business, information needs to circulate on networks, PCs, Web sites, and on individual computers. Inert, noncirculating data creates little wealth. The paradox derives from the conflict between the desire for commerce and the need for security, and it will bedevil security professionals in the twenty-first century.

The third paradox arises from the personality of the modern corporation. Warriors against industrial espionage confront businesses that are not perpetual, static entities. A protective client in January may not be the same client in April. Fluid in employees, investors, management, and in business objectives, twenty-first century businesses embrace protean, mercurial transformations. Last year's security plan becomes obsolete faster than you anticipate. Will the pace of obsolescence continue to quicken? Are monthly revisions in security plans going to be the norm?

We face a new reality. Businesses will become more virtual. Composed of changing alliances, new methods of organization, ephemeral personnel, they will tax any static approach to security measures. In large organizations keeping user groups and access control lists current for network services wavers between a near impossibility to a "major challenge" for information technology (IT) security professionals. Constantly changing numbers of workers and revisions in mission objectives renders access privileges for databases and networks to slip "out of sync" with organizational reality. Who are we? What are we? These pithy questions become more than rhetorical devices; they reflect the angst of trying to protect an organization with ever evolving frontiers.

Understanding the drumbeat of the company's march in near time and space, that dilemma remains the greatest challenge for twenty-first century security. Viewing contemporary businesses as anything less than chameleon results in tunnel vision and in defending an illusion. Two adversaries exist for the security practitioner: the industrial spy and the ever-changing client. Thinking about what the client was last month may not address the threat of today. Considering what the enterprise could be tomorrow becomes a necessary survival skill. The fourth paradox compels the security specialist to act like the Roman god Janus, looking both to the past and to the future. Obviously, having current action plans will always be necessary, but constant reevaluation on their effectiveness for tomorrow may be the new mandate.

The security professional's battle against industrial espionage faces increasing technological assaults. Consider these trends:

1. Information technology is moving toward Palm OS, Pocket PCs, and other hand-held computers. Proprietary data gets less centralized, harder to track and to protect behind a defensive perimeter.

2. The "office" wanes more virtual. Armed with a cellular telephone and a portable-computing device, the information worker has less of a need to conduct business at a central location on a regular basis. The line of defense becomes increasingly nebulous because a greater number of assets lie beyond physical security barriers or boundaries.

3. Self-sufficiency continues to grow among computer users. A plethora of information and software eases access to programming techniques and to database management. Users, even with the best intentions, may create information resources, which serve as a gold mine for the information predator. With little thought or concern, they carry these treasures on devices protected by less than ideal security.

4. Information channels diversify, becoming less controllable. Users, not bound by the company's email systems, networks, or telecommunications, define their own boundaries for access.

Instant messaging systems, cellular telephones, pocket computers, and wireless technologies create hidden realms for workers, and even for visitors to the company. Such users possess the ability to make up their own rules regarding exchange or release of information.

5. As the Internet attracts more commerce, this unparalleled information magnet grows; industrial spies enjoy previously arduous access to open sources with relative ease. This resource locates "the missing pieces," the economic, business, or regulatory facts in the public realm that fill in their intelligence gathering puzzle. With a well-defined shopping list, spies learn where to shop for sought-after sensitive information before ever penetrating the target. The business becomes an information supermarket where they know what is on "aisles 12 and 14B" before they arrive.

A BRIEF SCENARIO

Richard Jackson, a project manager with Computer Ventures International (our fictional firm), decides to load project management software on his hand-held PC. Since the hand-held connects by cabling to his desktop at work, he has a lightweight means to take work home, for synchronizing files changes between the two machines is a breeze. While the company has a policy against taking sensitive project files from the office, no one is going to check his pockets. With a "PC-on-the-go" he can work at the beach, on the patio, or in the study at his private club. Unfortunately, Richard's work habits come under the observation of an industrial spy. One day, while Richard's kicking up the surf at the beach, the spy borrows that pocket PC for a bit and copies the sensitive project files. Richard thought he protected the files with the password utility that came with the project management software. Leaving the pocket PC wrapped in a beach towel, he thought no one would notice it. Wrong on both counts, Richard's security measures fell far short. The beach towel was the first place the thief looked. And, the password was easy, for like most proprietary cryptographic products, it derived from a Vigenère square, old precomputer "crypto." Prior to the theft, a little research on the Internet taught the spy how to crack the password. Anyway, the password was "Carla," Richard's girl-friend, not too difficult to guess.

The virtual office usually lacks the physical security of a regular office location. Out of town, Richard drops into a copying center; he looks upon these outlets as offices away from home. He copies several documents for a presentation. As a part of his cleanup, he throws "old" or "obsolete" pages in the trash basket by the copier, not thinking any risk carries with the disposal. He picks up a fax at the copying center from the home office, and after reading the message, he tosses that piece of paper too. It was just an update on the "where and when" of the next day's meeting. Prior to leaving the center, Richard plops on a sofa in the waiting area and calls the office on his cellular telephone. He discusses with a co-worker the fax's contents and what the agenda of tomorrow's meeting will be. Several people within earshot hear the conversation. After the call, Richard heads back to his hotel. His behavior, while far from reckless, was sloppy as far as information security goes. Maybe he hasn't compromised some important data, maybe he has. Without secure telephone communications in a private area, without document shredding, who can really tell? Perhaps, the world was indifferent to Richard's data discards; hopefully, that is the case. But, we do know workers are out in the world every working day doing what Richard did in the copy center. All those little discards have to add up somewhere.

Richard often gets frustrated with the restrictions of the company's firewall. He feels it blocks access to sites necessary for his job. Also, it blocks people from sending him certain files. The firewall creates too many bottlenecks. As an act of self-empowerment, of self-sufficiency, he gets a laptop with a modem to provide his own Internet access, bypassing the company's network and firewall. He also does some company business using his own email hand-held device. Again, this email channel gives him flexibility and convenience. He has the ability to transmit and to receive emails outside of the company's normal network, affording him irresistible privacy.

Unfortunately, if Richard leaves his laptop turned on at night, someone may be able to get access to his proprietary files via the modem connection. His personal email channel may lead to him saying things, revealing sensitive information that wouldn't be allowed on the corporate channel, unless encrypted. Private channels created by workers only generate backdoors through the security perimeter.

Finding details about an employee like Richard isn't all that hard on the Internet for an industrial spy. A profile of Richard and his employer are available on a project management society's Web site. He has postings on newsgroups about technical questions stemming from his project management work. His published articles are available via Google and other search engines on the Internet. Building a background profile or dossier on a person like him, with a responsible job, forms a part of the industrial spy's stock-in-trade. The background data is useful in guessing passwords, in impersonating the individual during "social engineering," or in developing steppingstones to other more sensitive information.

THE REST OF THE BOOK

Will one person like Richard by himself alone create this much exposure for a company? Probably not, however, it takes only a few Richards, making minor mistakes, to cause sizeable information leaks. The prime directive of twentieth century security was: "Encircle your assets with barriers, locks, gates, and guards." Such an approach requires revision. Diffusion, dispersal, and mobility, the hallmarks of twenty-first century information, work against that model. Rather, we need security models that embrace the energy and the dynamic quality of our times.

In an age awash with free-flowing information, what should be our strategy? Our first step peers into the history of industrial espionage in America. The lessons from history reveal that most tricks spies employ are centuries old. By learning the tricks, the student of industrial espionage (IE) understands that today's techniques spin off from what's happened before in America and England since the sixteenth century. Corporate or industrial spying employs observation, knowledge, politics, and power as the fundamental attacks.

Observation techniques eyeball an industrial smokestack or look for the number of railcars on a track siding from a satellite image. Whatever outsiders see from the air, from space, or from across the street, tells a story, a more extensive story than most managers would imagine. Learning to see with a spy's eyes adds an invaluable tool to security's arsenal. Critical knowledge comes from effective observation. The text covers observation techniques in Chapters 1 and 4.

Knowledge techniques recognize that information builds upon information; one fact leads to another. The more a spy knows about a target, the easier the intelligence mission will be in getting the right information the first time. An effective spy does the homework prior to any target penetration. Building footholds with research beforehand creates leverage points against the target. Chapters 2 and 5 cover knowledge techniques such as competitive technical intelligence, patent analysis, and exploiting open information sources.

Politics and power techniques range from blackmail to bribery to seduction. Political moves involve changing alliances within a company or industry. Spies exploit political friction and turf wars to develop openings for attacks. Political strategies may also come into play in efforts to defuse or to maneuver around security efforts. Power works with either money or sex. Deception, however, also enters the power equation. If the holders of secrets can't be bribed or seduced into yielding secrets, perhaps they can be bamboozled into eagerly divulging sensitive matters. We'll examine all the perspectives of power and politics in industrial spying in Chapters 1 and 6.

Chapters 3, 4, and 5 relate the origins of industrial spying in England and America. The reader becomes familiar with techniques spies have used since the Age of Shakespeare. In fact one of the spies discussed will be an Elizabethan playwright and poet. The architect of intelligence gathering as an organized science will be a philosopher and courtier.

In Chapter 7 we'll discuss the traditional countermeasures that form the basis of American industrial security doctrine, but from the perspective of a spy. And, while this text advocates looking beyond these countermeasures to intelligence methods, the author by no means advocates abandoning physical security. Rather, the thoughtful employment of physical security, while recognizing its limitations, serves as the bedrock of the security profession.

Chapters 8 and 9 present supplemental methods to physical security. They focus on internal and external intelligence gathering. Finding out what is happening inside and outside of your organization may be the best defense against IE. Only by peering beyond the defensive perimeter, a defense, which served us well in the twentieth century but now needs redefinition, can we find ways to protect sensitive information along an increasingly undefined security border.

The main text concludes with Chapter 10 that discusses investigating IE cases. The focus is on the *Economic Espionage Act of 1996*. We'll concentrate on building evidence in these cases.

To aid the reader, at the end of the main text, there are a Chronology of Anglo-American industrial espionage, Chapter Notes, and a Master Checklist. The Chronology summarizes how the craft of commercial intelligence evolved from Renaissance England to Modern America. In the Chapter Notes, I amplify the main text and explain where certain perspectives arose. The Master Checklist summarizes all of the key security actions suggested by the text.

DISCUSSION

1. Consider ways where cryptographic measures can fall short. Cite articles, books, or Web sites to support your findings.
2. How does the historical perspective of industrial espionage aid in the training of a security specialist?
3. List four methods an industrial spy could employ to penetrate your company. Be specific in your answer.

FOR FURTHER READING

Bruce Schneier's *Secrets & Lies* (John Wiley & Sons, Inc., 2000) offers a nontraditional approach to information security. While a cryptography expert, Schneier does not see encryption as a cure-all for security problems. He suggests identifying probable avenues of attack a perpetrator might use as a means to enhance the security of information assets.

Chapter 1

THE FACTORY VISIT (OBSERVATION)

Observing better than Sherlock Holmes is an industrial spy's great-est asset, for as the master of detection would agree, mere seeing never catches the latent truth. By observing, the spy penetrates beyond the surface meaning of people, places, events, or things. For example, a tourist visiting a chocolate factory doesn't give much thought to the parking lot around the building's exterior. A trained intelligence spe-cialist counts the number of parking spaces. He or she notes whether drivers park vehicles outside the existing lot's bounds. This overflow may indicate an expanding business. A rough idea of the incomes the business generates derives from mentally averaging the workers' vehi-cles' years and by noting the vehicles' makes. Do the same for the man-agers' vehicles. (Managers' vehicles usually have reserved spots next to the plant's exterior walls.)

In addition to automobiles, the intelligence gatherer will record the arrivals and departures of commercial trucks. The trucks' logos reveal the identities of suppliers and vendors. And, the pace of commercial traffic may indicate the tempo of production at the facility.

Jotting down license plate numbers from the management parking spaces aids in identifying who those people are. Such information, tying the person to their vehicle, may be useful in latter surveillance. The markings on boxes and crates stored outside of the facility often yields clues on what materials or parts the manufacturing processes use. In other words, trained eyes learn a great deal about a business even before they enter the doors.

Wait a minute, you say, and point out that none of what's been described above is illegal. Why is it spying if it is not illegal? The text takes a broad view of industrial spying. Whether an activity is legal or ethical or even socially acceptable really doesn't mean much. If your proprietary secrets leak out legally, your client still has lost an asset.

While intelligence specialists may spend many hours debating what is permissible business intelligence and what is industrial espionage, we don't waste time dividing the commercial intelligence community into white and black hats. They are all after your client's inside information. The smarter ones realize legal boundaries exist, and they wisely stay behind them by using legal and, depending upon one's definition, ethical methods. But, as a security professional, you need to look at the information security issue from all perspectives. The criminals you'll work to catch and prosecute. Your client may seek criminal and civil remedies against the parties that hired them. The others you will try to block in every legitimate way you can. Just because they agree not to break the law or to violate obvious ethical standards doesn't equate to them being entitled to your sensitive information. If the information were easy to get, their clients wouldn't hire them to do the business intelligence work. And, you are allowed to cloak and hide (by legal means) as much as you can from these people.

A factory tour takes several forms. An industrial spy may simply walk into a plant, which has low security, posing as a prospective employee, a graduate student writing a research paper, a utility meter reader, or as a vendor. If construction is occurring at the site, a spy may don a hard hat, work clothes and gloves, and wear a utility belt. By blending in, the operative can wander around the site asking questions, observing, and even taking photographs.

When greater security exists, the spy may join a public tour of the facility, if available. Sometimes such tours serve up an information buffet for an observant intelligence gatherer. Doing research beforehand enhances the tour; knowing what to look for enables the spy to focus in on critical details in limited time. Library and Internet research, interviews with industry experts and former employees, and discussions with suppliers and vendors constitute good preparation. If public tours aren't available, the spy may try to join a vendor or a service provider's firm, which permits regular access to the premises. The copy machine technician, for example, gets to see a lot, to hear a great deal, and even to handle documents.

Effective spies know what they are after. The shopping list usually includes:

1. Identifying parts and materials used in manufacture. (Also identifying sources of supply.)
2. Understanding industrial processes and manufacturing steps.
3. The amounts of raw materials and finished goods on hand.
4. Proprietary techniques, formulas, and control systems used.
5. Software and computer systems employed.
6. Production schedules, shifts, and the number of workers employed. The number of workers in each job classification.
7. Production records, reports, lab notes, or engineering reports and drawings.
8. Machinery or equipment used.
9. Physical dimensions and layout of the plant.
10. Physical characteristics of support areas such as incoming roads, railroads, waterways, docks, parking lots, and employee facilities such as the cafeteria and break areas.
11. Financial records pertaining to manufacture.
12. Marketing records or sales records pertaining to production or manufacture.
13. Any production problems at the site.
14. Any construction in progress at the site.
15. Security measures in place at the facility.

If the target contains a research facility, then the intelligence effort will seek:

A. Relevant contents of research databases.
B. The identity and job descriptions of key research staff.
C. Project plans, descriptions, and progress reports.
D. Research supplies, materials, and equipment used.
E. Project managers' reports.
F. Costs or cost accounting records associated with projects.
G. Any prototypes, models, or preproduction goods created by research efforts.

Rarely will any of these targets be lying on a desk with large arrows pointing to them saying "Valuable Secrets." Instead, the industrial spy learns to gather bits and pieces to build a larger picture. She rivets them together into coherent intelligence. Constructing the picture defines the craft of intelligence, a passionate endeavor requiring cunning and filled with intellectual challenge.

The security professional's response demands equal passion and the ability to stretch one's mind. Often, the inner commitment required struggles against bureaucratic inertia and politics. For example, the company may remain committed to public tours of the plant despite information security risks. Many corporate officers consider such programs good public relations. A resourceful security specialist, thinking and seeing with a hawk's predatory eye, must develop ways to blunt the spy's vision and to cloak any clues the tour affords.

Intelligence gathering is a continuum. A plant tour may reveal small clues, moderate clues, or big ones. Security's aim seeks to keep the collection efforts on the small end of the continuum. Defending everything may be impossible or simply not feasible. Keeping any yardage gained to short distances is a reasonable protection strategy. Some information leaks will occur, especially if your business has size and complexity. Placing roadblocks to deter a spy from climbing high on the information tree remain within the realm of effective action.

A tour of the plant may allow an outsider to see from the established path processing vats and connecting lines. However, placing all labeling for the vats and lines on the worker's side and not on the path's side reduces any information telegraphed during the tour. Many such cloaking strategies are available and inexpensive; one just needs to see from a rogue's viewpoint. (See "Cloaking" in Chapter 4.) Walk through your plant with the operations manager, and point out clues a visitor discovers when doing a "friendly tour." Such a step will build a relationship with management, and it demonstrates that you are paying attention to details.

MCDONNELL DOUGLAS 1993

Plant 85 in Columbus, Ohio possessed machines to manufacture Titan and MX missiles. Known as "five-axis profilers," these machines held the interest of CATIC, an acronym for the Chinese Aero-Technology Import and Export Corporation. The offer of other business, highly desirable contracts, enabled the CATIC team to tour the McDonnell Douglas facility. Armed with their notepads, film cameras, and video cameras, they received and captured a good technical portrait of advanced American technology with both military and commercial applications.

Some historians of business intelligence, such as John J. Fialka in *War by Other Means: Economic Espionage in America* (W.W. Norton and Co., 1977), see the McDonnell Douglas factory visit and the subsequent business deals as a prime example of American business myopia. The desire for short-term profits overrides long-term strategy. Having profits today becomes the primary concern, even though it may jeopardize business in the future. Whether you are still in business in a not too distant tomorrow is something to worry about in the coming years.

The labor union at McDonnell Douglas worried more about the technology transfer threat than the company's management. While McDonnell Douglas's management team arguably did conduct business with the Chinese because it was in the company's best interest, they have ignored common sense dangers perceived by the average worker. Frequently in American business, the rank and file workers become more tied to the company than the management. To management and the stockholders, the corporation exists to generate wealth, and the quicker, the better. To the workers the company represents a way and a means of life. So, the labor union had vision when it expressed concerns about the Chinese running around asking questions and taking pictures amidst proprietary, high-tech machinery.

The McDonnell Douglas incident demonstrates that intelligence gathering need not be surreptitious. In fact, what the Chinese did was quite legal. Putting an offer of money on the table can open many guarded doors. Adversaries with a willingness (to borrow a phrase from the CBS television series, *Survivor*) "to outplay, to outwit, and to outlast" can steal many secrets from American companies. A strange irony in American security practice is, despite a security's professional's best efforts to keep spies out, that same professional may end up as one of the tour guides to "visitors" who have bought or promised their way in the door. (Of course, not all potential customers are spies. But, any business has to be extremely careful on who gains access to sensitive, proprietary information. Outsiders that get access must be held accountable with nondisclosure and confidentiality agreements.)

Technological complacency also works against budgets and extensive security actions for information security measures. The thinking goes, "Even if we lose some technological edge, there's innovation coming down the road every day to make up the difference." Unfortunately, industrial spies begin feeding far upstream. They stick their noses not only into production facilities but into universities and research centers too. They prey upon ideas at every step in the invention cycle. Protect what you got at every phase. Any time outsiders cross your threshold; your level of concern should rise. Despite any announced intentions, regardless of who sponsors them in upper management, no matter what carrots dangle before the board of directors, viewing visitors with caution is not imbibing paranoia. True, America still has an aerospace industry, but so do the Chinese. We should not be in business to build our competitor's businesses, whether they are foreign or domestic.

TREDEGAR IRON WORKS 1861

The Confederate States of America (CSA) had to make war with limited resources. Lacking the industrial infrastructure of the North, the CSA looked to imaginative solutions in defending the Southland. One technological area open to exploitation was submersible or submarine warfare. To protect the South's numerous rivers and harbors against infiltration by the U.S. Navy, submersibles offered a mobile minefield underwater. And, submarines could provide an offensive capability against the naval blockade of Southern ports.

Named for an iron works in Wales, the Tredegar Iron Works in Richmond, Virginia provided the CSA with the resources to manufacture ironclads, and submarines. Heavily protected from both military attack and the prying eyes of Union spies, Tredegar produced nearly 11,000 field and siege cannon during the Civil War. Its rolling mills produced armor plating for ironclads such as the *Merrimac*.

Allan Pinkerton's Union intelligence service understood the threat that Tredegar and its ability to make below the surface warships posed. In fact, General McClellan's plan was to move up the peninsula bordered by the James and York rivers and move on Richmond and the Tredegar Iron Works. But, riverine submersibles and ironclads like the *Merrimac* created serious problems for an expeditionary force. Somehow, the Union had to get someone inside Tredegar to find out what was mere gossip and what was a real threat.

Mrs. E.H. Baker was Pinkerton's choice to penetrate Tredegar. Although she lived in the North, she had friends in Richmond. With some carefully planned correspondence to those friends, she arranged to have an invitation from them to come to Richmond in November 1861.

After arriving in Richmond, she made the social circuit of home visits, afternoon teas, and evening social events. Once she created a social comfort zone with her Confederate hosts, she managed to arrange escorts around Richmond by various CSA officers. Eventually these tours included the Tredegar Iron Works. Playing the role of the Southern belle, she was able to witness work on a submarine. Allowed to look inside the vessel, she made mental notes on its construction. When she was alone, she was able to transfer her observations to paper and to create drawings later conveyed to Pinkerton.

The submarine Mrs. Baker saw probably was the one designed by W.G. Cheeney, a master in the Confederate navy. It probably never went into service due to an unanticipated opportunity the Union spy had to witness submersibles in action. (A submersible floats just below the waterline or surface with a snorkel above water to supply a continuous airflow, while a submarine moves well under the surface.) Mrs. Baker witnessed a gray-green submersible on one of Richmond's rivers engage in detonating a "submarine battery" which was a water-based mine.

With the knowledge of stationary submersibles armed with mines being in Southern rivers, the Union Navy developed countermeasures: usually fouling the snorkel apparatus. The submersibles didn't have much effect on the Union Navy. While the *Hunley* did see some action near Charleston S.C. late in the war, the South never made a sizable commitment to submarine warfare. Intelligence gathered by Pinkerton's operative probably contributed, along with the considerable loss of life among the CSA's submariners, to the South's ultimately feeble effort.

LOWELL NATIONAL HISTORICAL PARK

Lowell, Massachusetts was the birthplace of American industry. The National Park Service maintains an historical site in Lowell to commemorate the role Lowell played in making the United States an industrial power. When touring the park, I saw exhibits on the founding of Lowell as a center of the textile industry. Situated on the Merrimac River, Lowell had a natural energy source for its textile mills. Workers in the mills were primarily women; known as the "Lowell Girls," they came from rural areas in New England to try the new way of life in industrialism.

When visiting Lowell NHP, it becomes quite clear that the textile mills are long dead in Massachusetts. What remains in the park are some restored buildings, but also many that are decayed, dilapidated, and mere echoes of a robust past. One of Lowell's great lessons is that industrial strength disappears when not cherished and guarded. A resource that constantly struggles against competition, our industrial base can fall prey to clever observation. The person who founded Lowell, Francis Cabot Lowell, was a masterful observer, who noted enough of British accomplishments in textile manufacture to transplant the industry to America.

Between 1811 and 1813, Lowell lived in England. He visited textile mills in Scotland and Derbyshire. His interest went well beyond that of a tourist. He was researching the British textile industry. The Cartwright loom became his target. Extensive mental notes enabled him to bring back the plans for the loom. Even though British Customs extensively searched him before he returned to America, they found no plans or drawings.

Upon returning to America, Lowell engaged the services of a mechanic. Based upon his research, Lowell built a scale model of the Cartwright loom. From that model, he was able to construct working looms for the mills of Lowell. Francis Cabot Lowell was a master of business intelligence exploiting the "factory tour" technique to create a whole new industry in America. He used the intellectual capital of Britain to give America a tremendous boost in building an industrial society.

Lowell didn't commit burglary or even simple larceny in the common-law sense of the terms. He "borrowed" other people's ideas because they didn't guard their trade secrets effectively. So, Lowell started a tradition that continued with Allan Pinkerton and goes on today, thanks to our competitors from Asia and Europe. They are out doing what America used to do: roam the industrial world for ideas on how things can be improved. America went from being an intellectual debtor nation to one that lends out its intellectual capital on an unpaid basis.

No sense of fair play exists in industrial espionage. If your proprietary data is easy to access, your competitors will take advantage of the deficiency in your security. So, being wary of what outsiders can see, hear, touch, smell, or even taste when they visit your premises should be a cause for very real concern.

DISCUSSION

The text's primary aim is practical advice. While it explores the historical and broader issues of industrial espionage, arming the security specialist with concrete suggestions remains at the core. The Discussion sections will vary in length, sometimes long and other times just a list of questions or ideas for further exploration. But, always they will strive to connect the readers to the realities of fighting industrial or corporate espionage in the business world.

In this chapter, the reader obtained insight into how the "factory tour" is one of the oldest pieces of IE's trade craft. It has been around a long time and will remain on the spy scene in the twenty-first century.

A good exercise for any security professional involves playing the thief's role. Correcting information clues available to a spy in a walk-through of your facility, that's the challenge. See with the information predator's eyes. Only after looking for what a thief seeks will you hide, cloak, move, and misdirect successfully. Ira Winkler in his *Corporate Espionage* (Prima Publishing, 1997) suggests a facilities walk-through as an excellent tool for detecting vulnerabilities in information security. He mentions looking at employees' desktops, trying locks, checking computer terminals and keyboards for notes, and examining documents left next to the copying machines.

I can echo Mr. Winkler's suggestions based upon a late night inspection I did of a computer company's offices. The door to the CEO's suite was unlocked. I was able to walk in and read his mail. I could note proprietary data written on his whiteboard. His pocket PC device was available if I wanted to download its contents.

When I went to the cubicles for the Finance Department, I found papers that identified the company's foreign banks, complete with account numbers and balances. Keyboards had passwords or logins taped underneath. In one office nearby, travel documents and itineraries were in open view. In another office, the Internet manager's personal and business weekly planner was available to be read and copied.

This litany of discoveries could go on for several pages, but the point is keeping one's eyes open for targets and thinking like a rogue define the modern security professional. As an exercise, without breaking any laws or rules of your organization, go through your premises after regular hours. (Obtain management's consent before doing the search.) Make a list of the following:

1. What is visible on blackboards, whiteboards, and calendars?
2. Documents found around the copying machine and the nearby trash basket.
3. Can you gain access to labs and testing areas? How about the computer operations center?
4. In production areas, are equipment, materials, and workstations labeled in a way that gives clues to outsiders as to what is going on? Can they build the steps in the production (manufacturing) process from the signage?
5. Visit the outside trash bin or dumpster. Are intact, legible documents in the trash? How about computer media? If you run the computer media such as floppy disks on a machine, what files do you find?

From this data collection effort plan an information attack on your organization. In the plan, devise a list of targets and a timetable for securing the desired information. Such exercises on a regular basis will not only improve your security plan, but they will also cultivate your awareness as a security professional.

Being aware of the tactics of the information predator is essential. The prime operative factor will always be the ability to blend in. If the predator can join a public tour, they will. If your business has construction going on, they will dress as a construction worker complete with a hardhat. Other tactics include masquerading as a service vendor, a cleaning worker, or an authorized visitor such as a consultant, intern, or prospective employee.

An excellent mind experiment involves brainstorming methods and techniques to interdict information predators. Devise ways to prevent them from blending in once inside the security perimeter. Try to insure they can't learn much even if they wander around. Think beyond just issuing badges. A jingle or mantra doesn't come to mind to summarize the overall response, but "cloak obvious clues" and "make sure visitors can't roam" sound close to the right admonitions. How often do you walk through your business identifying visual clues and seeing that they get covered up or removed? (If the temperature and pressure in a holding tank are a part of your manufacturing trade secrets, stenciling those values on the tank's side doesn't help preserve the secret.) Do visitors get challenged once they get past the badge-issuing ritual at the security officer's station? Be creative, and develop tactful, polite ways to keep tabs on visitors within your company. (Internal checkpoints, color coding schemes for different areas of the building to restrict badge use, video surveillance cameras, building escorts, and pagers for visitors that double as tracers, all of these tools maintain internal coverage on visitors.)

Power issues are another factor in the factory or office visit. In the McDonnell Douglas case, the Chinese exercised financial power, the promise of new business. Probably, as a security professional, you can't block people from the businesses that promise new opportunities for the company. That practice doesn't make much business sense. However, you can explain to your management that prospective customers can masquerade as "partners" and end up being spies. Rolling out the red carpet doesn't include the dropping of security standards. Encourage management to obtain confidentiality and nondisclosure agreements from prospective customers. Make sure measures are in place to monitor visitors while they are on the premises.

Another issue to consider is sexual power. Mrs. Baker at Tredegar, while she didn't have sex with or try to seduce her hosts, she still exploited Southern notions of femininity to her advantage. They did not suspect her because of her gender. She was glad to be escorted by Southern gentlemen. They were not threatened by showing her sensitive places, things, and events.

Sexual charisma, whether by a female or a male, can be very difficult to resist. After all, as a force that speaks to our innermost nature and drives, it can be most attractive and disarming. At one extreme, sexual recruiting of key personnel can result in sexual relationships that exist solely to pump individuals for information. Richard Marcinko's *Rogue Warrior: Detachment Bravo* (Pocket Star Books, 2002) novel describes how a member of the Navy SEAL team uses a sexual relationship with an intelligence officer in an embassy to gain information. The tactic is ancient trade craft. And, anyone can succumb to this intrigue.

Perhaps even more dangerous are the subtle forms of sexual power. An affair may not be necessary. If your employee finds a visitor attractive, they may bend the rules for that individual or extend courtesies not given to others. And sometimes, all it takes is a slight bending of security roles to make an industrial spy's mission successful.

The only real defense against sexual power plays is education of the work force. All visitors need equal treatment regardless of their sex, their attractiveness, or lack of attractiveness. Employees need to be wary of relationships where the partner is too interested in the employee's job. These principles should become a part of any security education program.

OBSERVATION (EXERCISES)

A security professional must be a keen observer. The following exercises may help in developing this skill. Observing is more than recognizing what is in the current range of vision. The ability to see beyond the evidence at hand and to look behind the scenes becomes essential.

1. Visit a locale that you have no previous experience with its content or organization. Stretch yourself, and go to a restaurant, to a nightclub, or to a place of business that is culturally or ethnically different from your background. Make mental notes of your surroundings, and then create a list of actions you could take to blend in better on a return visit.

2. Do a security survey of a secured facility that allows limited public access. This facility could be a courthouse, a police station, or a financial institution. Without breaking any laws or compromising the facility's security, make a list of actions you could take to bypass or compromise the facility's physical security.

3. Imagine you are a corporate spy that needs to hide some stolen documents for pickup later. Identify three "spy drop" sites within your company where the documents could go undetected for 48 hours. Then, find three drop sites in public places like parks, bus stations, shopping malls, and so on.

4. Walk through your parking lot at work or school. Without entering anyone's vehicle, make note of the visual clues on or inside the vehicle that tell you about the employee's personal or professional life.

5. Observe commercial deliveries at a business. Use binoculars if you wish. Make notes on what you can tell about the company's activities from the trucks making the deliveries and from the goods visible on the loading dock.

6. Do a factory visit at a company whose line of business is something you know little about. Make notes about the clues you find that reveal how things are done or how processes work. Then do some research on that industry. How much does the research enhance what you observed? What kind of prior research would you need to do in the future to improve your powers of observation at an unfamiliar business?

FOR FURTHER READING

1. *Rogue Warrior: Detachment Bravo* by Richard Marcinko and John Weisman (Pocket Star Books, 2002) Marcinko may be a man of action, but his thrillers are actually thoughtful discussions on how to gather intelligence and to provide security.

2. *Providing Executive Protection* by Richard W. Kobetz, editor (Executive Protection Institute, 1991) The chapter "Terrorism: The Female Diversion," by Deborah M. Galvin, has good insights on sexual power as a tool of espionage or terror.

3. "Ask Me No Secrets, I'll Tell You No Lies" by Ronald Mendell (*Security Management,* May 1994, Vol. 38, No. 5) The article contains an overview of cloaking techniques and a profile of an information predator.

4. "Observation Still Matters" by Ronald Mendell (*P.I. Magazine,* Spring 1996, Vol. 9, No. 1) An article about increasing your powers of observation.

5. *Corporate Espionage* by Ira Winkler (Prima Publishing, 1997) The book contains a superb overview about how corporate spies will penetrate your company.

Chapter 2

KNOWLEDGE

Knowledge creates leverage. Facts, like pyramid stones, build upon each other. The algebra of industrial spying allows the intelligence gatherer to calculate "C" if "A" and "B" become known. Knowledge-based attacks depend upon source information, data usually found in the public sector. The intelligence analyst bootstraps that information to generate inferences about a target.

In addition, research into publicly available facts from government records, press reports, and industry publications establishes stepping stones to create a pathway for penetrating the company. Knowing what to look for completes 75% percent of the spy's job. Research prior to direct intelligence operations draws a map so the industrial spy does have to operate in the dark.

As we indicated in the Introduction, combating industrial espionage is never free of paradox. Companies possess valuable information without being aware of its existence. Drowning in a sea of facts, data everywhere, unable to identify patterns in their own information, they miss opportunities that refining and filtering this information into knowledge would provide. By gaining access to a company's databases, a spy may be able to mine those information resources for treasures, assets the target has yet to realize. (See the section below, "SQL and Data Mining" for more on this topic.)

The basis of any intelligence effort against a technology company will be open source Competitive Technical Intelligence (CTI). This effort depends upon research and analysis techniques. Such methods seek to identify a company's progress within its technological sector and what resources it can bring to future endeavors. CTI determines a company's standing within a technological family. For example, among biotechnology firms, ranking the company on Alzheimer's disease research concerning medications may depend on several factors. The size of the research budget, the number of drugs developed, the estimated time left for the regulatory approval by the FDA, all of these factors enter into evaluating the company's research standing or posture.

CTI turns the industrial espionage specialist into a detective. As a detective, the specialist pursues clues in the technical literature regarding the innovative pulse of the target. The uses of CTI involve providing technical descriptions of existing or emerging technologies or identifying shifts in technological change.

Before any intelligent data gathering can begin, the specialist first must understand the industry and the target's role in that industry. The spy's client generally wants to gain an upper hand in developing emerging technologies. True, stealing current technology helps a business compete in today's market. And, a considerable amount of industrial espionage effort goes in that direction.

But, to compete over the long run, however, requires putting one's ear to the technological rail and listening for approaching trains bringing innovation. Anyone with access to a copying machine or a floppy disk can purloin today's secrets. Stealing tomorrow's intellectual capital, however, demands some finesse and careful research. Recognizing shifts in technology, transitions from one line of research to another, where substitute or competing technologies become available, requires database analysis, technical literature research, and even Delphi polling. (A Delphi poll entails interviewing experts in the field on their opinions regarding the future of the technology.)

Assessing market influences on a target's technology forms another important task for the intelligence analyst. While this activity may fall more directly into business or marketing intelligence, espionage agents still have a role. Open sources document changes in government regulation or in consumer preferences. Both are factors affecting the market environment. Yet, assessing a target's intentions, how it will respond to the changes requires inside information. Learning a competitor's intentions forms the crux of commercial spying. Judging a capability is easy, relatively speaking. But, to know what an adversary plans to do with a capability, there's the rub.

The shopping list for the technological spy would then include:

A. Identifying emerging technologies that the target has within its organization. (Just because the target possesses a nifty technology doesn't mean they will exploit its potential. Xerox gave Apple the idea for the graphical interface that became Apple's operating system. (Xerox failed to exploit the potential.)

B. Recognizing shifts in technology and their impact on the target. Is the target working on research projects likely to succeed or will they be dead ends? (Delphi polling may help in this analysis.)

C. Comparing substitute or competing technologies and predict the target's response to them. (Will the target stay on its own path or will it adopt other points of view in developing a new technology?)

D. Recognizing marketing influences on the target's research programs.

Producing actionable intelligence becomes crucial. A spy's client has to be able to make decisions based upon reliable intelligence gathering. If the intelligence product doesn't support decision making, then little reason exists for the intelligence effort. To produce actionable intelligence, the industrial spy should: (1) Observe the target's actions in committing resources of supplies, equipment, and people toward specific objectives, (2) Gain a feel for management's inclinations by interviewing employees, suppliers, and vendors, (3) Assess technological progress from technical journals and the trade press, (4) Obtain the target's marketing and research project reports and plans, and (5) Finish the mosaic by gathering expert opinion on where the company is going, and will they be successful?

The key counter-strategies for security, in order to dampen these efforts, involve cloaking critical operations, training employees to beware of social engineering, and restricting access to marketing and research plans or reports. Cloaking employs the complexity of a large organization to security's advantage. Hide sensitive production or research operations, or, at least render ambiguous what is going on. Questioning of employees by people they don't know, which seeks to learn intentions or plans, must raise suspicion. Train employees that they are a first line of defense regarding moves against the company and maintain strict access controls over sensitive planning documents by locking them up (whether physically or electronically) and by establishing chain of custody records to track possession of the materials. (See Chapter 4, "Cloaking," Chapter 5, "Sources of Information" on social engineering, and Chapter 6, "Trade Secret Theft.")

In addition to technological perspectives, corporate spies don't overlook the target's business standing. This organizational analysis includes:

A. Understanding patterns of business activity. When is the company more active? How is the increased activity related to the company's progress?
B. Identifying the strengths and weaknesses of the target. (These factors, whether positive or negative, may be financial resources, organizational capabilities, or logistical abilities. For example, a company may possess financial strength relative to its competitors but may lack the physical plant to bring a new product to manufacture.)
C. Reviewing a target's past performance financially and in meeting production schedules to project future trends.

In other words, corporate spies seek information along two channels: the business' standing (organizational analysis) and the intellectual capital available for plunder (Competitive Technical Analysis, CTI). Either body of knowledge affords considerable advantage to a spy's client. Access to other company's intellectual capital allows a competitor to shorten product development cycles, to cut research costs, and to counterattack with their own marketing plans based upon the target's secrets. A thorough knowledge of a competitor's business affords the client the opportunity to campaign where the target is weak. And perhaps, it allows the spy's client to recruit suppliers, vendors, and customers away from the target.

Chapters 4 and 5 will focus on organizational or business intelligence. The remainder of this chapter concentrates on CTI. By reviewing the open sources available, the reader learns the overt side of business intelligence. Yet, the same sources may constitute the "homework" necessary prior to an industrial spy's covert operations. "Black" covert activity rarely will be effective without advance "white" overt research.

Even though, however, we normally focus on the covert, illegal side of business intelligence, still learning the whole intelligence process is critical. Professional spies study their targets before making a move. Study the company you seek to protect. Put down your corporate eyeglasses, and peer through a spy's binoculars. Immerse yourself in the spy's perspective, whether the source is "white" or clandestine in origin. When you think like the enemy, maybe you can slip a few steps ahead.

TREES AND SEEDS

What then are the basic sources for CTI? Scientific and technical research encompasses vast regions. Thinking about the research enterprise as a tree helps to sort through a dense thicket of facts. A tree generates, of course, from a seed. As the tree grows, it develops major branches and then a multitude of smaller branches. But, by concentrating on first the seed and then on the main branches, the evolution of concepts and disciplines becomes clearer.

The first steps at a CTI effort are monitoring "seed" or "root" journals. Some of those key publications include:

1. Cybermetrics (http://www.cindoc.csic.es/cybermetrics/cybermetrics.html)
2. Communications of the ACM (http://www.acm.org/pubs/periodicals/cacm/)
3. International Journal of Innovation Management (http://www.worldscinet.com/ijim/ijim.shtml)
4. Journal of the American Society for Information Science and Technology (http://www.asis.org/Publications/Jasis/jasis.hmtl)

These are starting points for reviewing what is going on in technological innovation. Additional publications focus on highly specialized disciplines such as biotechnology, the chemical industry, or aerospace. Gateways to resources or publications in those areas are: (1) For biotechnology, "Biovista" (http://www.biovista.com/pf-rs.asp), (2) For chemistry, "Chemical News and Intelligence" (http://www.cnionline.com), and (3) For aerospace, "Aerospace Browser" (http://www.aerospacebrowser.com/).

The seed publications cover both general and specific innovation activities in various disciplines. An intelligence analyst focuses on areas where references to the target's activity surface in the literature. This information acts as a "heads up" for what is going on in a research discipline. Not only does this information help to define an industrial spy's campaign, what lines of inquiry to pursue, but it also helps in identifying potential targets, companies in the know.

Our intent here is not to make the reader a research scientist. Rather, acquainting the student of industrial espionage with a spy's "homework" makes one aware how knowledge-based attacks build footholds in the target's defenses. The more a spy knows prior to entering a company, the less he or she will stumble or fumble around in locating the right information. Starting with general publications and journals, the spy moves to more specific literature in the target's discipline. This effort defines research communities. Members of those communities will be scientists and technical experts who are key players in the field.

Before we move on, let's clarify how a researcher communicates information about his or her research. The following information paths are available to a researcher:

1. Lab notebooks.
2. Entries to internal research databases.
3. Internal email with other workers.
4. Memorandums and reports to company management. Possibly some internal company publications.
5. Open source company publications such as the annual report.
6. Open source trade, technical, or scientific magazines and journals.
7. Speeches or presentations to professional societies. Testimony before governmental bodies.
8. External email with other colleagues in the field.
9. Postings on Web sites, newsgroups, or electronic bulletin boards.
10. Profiles or interviews for the science or technical press, or general science articles written by the researcher.

Hopefully, from their employer's standpoint, researchers will keep proprietary data confined to items 1-4. Items 5-10 may contain general information sufficient to enable the researcher to carry out his or her job. Communicating general information or ideas to outsiders enhances the researcher's professional standing without compromising proprietary data.

From a spy's perspective items 1-4 hold the real treasure, but accessing that data directly may not be possible. However, information contained in items 5-10 may answer many questions or at least act as pointers to where other answers may be. A knowledge-based attack will look to the following:

1. Identify research relevant to the client's needs. And, who at the target is doing that research. (The spy who has done her homework knows where to go shopping.)
2. Determine which research communities are the most productive. (The spy can concentrate on places that offer the greatest yield.)
3. Identify who the key players are within the target. (This sifting out process narrows the field of employees that require background research and monitoring.)
4. Form a strategy for intelligence gathering against the target. (A penetration plan may not be necessary if all the required intelligence can be gathered from open sources. Or, preliminary intelligence efforts will reduce the need for internal operations within the target and minimize the risk of detection or exposure.)
5. Gather clues or partial information as to the contents of items 1-4. (Uncovering one fact makes it easier to discover other information. It is like finding stepping stones across a pond or a creek. Once one learns the geography, navigating a path to the desired information becomes easier.)

Other than seed publications, what are the additional open sources that a spy or an intelligence analyst may consult for CTI? Here are some suggestions:

• Commercial databases like Dialog®, LexisNexis™, and Dialog's Profound.
• Patent literature.
• Trade and industry journals.
• Dialog's NewsRoom.
• Science magazines such as the *Scientific American* and *Science.* (For more science magazines, consult these Web sites: http://newsdirectory.com/news/magazine/science and http://sciencepage.org/mags.htm.
• Abstracts of technical meetings. Online databases available on CDROM.
• Science databases. (For listings of science databases, see these Web sites: http://www.nrc.ca/irap/lifesciences/english.html, http://

www.internets.com/sscience.htm, http://www.internets.com/
sscilink.htm.
- Testimony before state and federal regulatory agencies.
- Reports on the results of research grants.
- Company annual reports.
- SEC filings.
- Trend studies by industry analysts.
- Investment analysts' reports.
- Directories and biographical encyclopedias for background material on scientists and researchers.
- Classified ads for scientific or research positions.

This list will never be all encompassing, because an intelligence gatherer's imagination and resourcefulness has no limits. Virtually any printed or electronic source becomes a tool for assembling the intelligence puzzle. For example, from a biographical encyclopedia, the analyst learns the college and the year of graduation for a targeted researcher. By consulting the college yearbook, the analyst discovers the names of some close classmates who were in the Physics Society with the target. She runs those names on a physics articles database. And, she finds articles written by those individuals on topics related to the target's interests.

A check of the current telephone directory for the target's locale reveals a few of the target's associates from college live nearby. Past telephone directories confirm that these associates have lived in the area for several years. Posing as a freelance science writer, the spy contacts these associates for background regarding the target's research. During the telephone interviews, the "writer" gains insights into the target's research because the associates have frequent contact with the target. They feel at ease and may reveal information that would not ordinarily be forthcoming from the target himself. Knowledge aids in such oblique attacks against targets.

TECHNICAL INTELLIGENCE

The types of activity for technical intelligence include:

1. Literature searches via commercially available databases.

2. Patent searches.
3. Attending science and technology conferences.
4. Reverse engineering of products. Taking them apart to see how they work (which is legal to do). In fact, a product's claim to be a trade secret may be nullified if it is easy to reverse engineer by ordinary means. (See Chapter 10 about trade secrets.)
5. Competitive benchmarking. Seeing how the company's technology stands in relation to competitors.
6. Competitor assessments. Interviewing competitors of the targeted business can do this. Or, interviewing experts in the field can also produce an assessment. Interviewing several experts can constitute a "Delphi Poll" regarding the consensus of expert opinion on the target's technological strengths and weaknesses.
7. Analyze the competitive environment from industry analysts' reports, business publications, and so on.
8. Segment the experts. This technique creates a list of critical questions that need answers. Rather than call on one expert or even a target to answer them, the questions are parsed out in separate interviews. No one gets the same questions or a lot of inquiries. So, no one becomes unduly guarded or suspicious because an interviewer is asking "too many questions."

Patents and technology intelligence requires an additional note. A patent is a technology indicator. By filing a patent, someone is trying to protect an innovation. However, few innovations stand outright by themselves. Most innovations are improvements upon what others have done. Generally, a new patent will make references to antecedent patents. A patent referred to by numerous later patents is a core technology.

- Patents analysis, as done by CTI analysts, covers four areas:
- Counting the number of patents in a particular discipline.
- Measuring the level of patent activity within a discipline. How many patents over what period of time?
- Determining the core technology. This analysis also can look at what could be up and coming new core technologies.
- Identifying inventors. Again, this analysis discloses key scientists or technical experts in a field.

Whether derived from patents, newspaper articles, or magazine articles, "information universes" emanate from the security professional's company into the public arena. When properly collected, sifted, and analyzed, the collected information generates actionable intelligence for a competitor. And, it can provide stepping-stones for a spy into your business. Open sources may help in identifying avenues of attack on the company. These knowledge-based attacks include:

1. Building background information on the targeted business. For example, if you learn who the key vendors are, you may be able to penetrate the target via the vendor. (Placing operatives with the vendor, compromising the vendors weaker IT security and accessing the targets.)
2. Building background data on key employees.
3. Gather enough data on the business to allow expert analysis.
4. Answer the intelligence analyst's critical questions by open source research techniques alone, which is completely legal. And, there is not much that security can do about this issue after the fact. Being aware of what is available in the public sector, however, may assist security in planning cloaking actions in the future. Awareness requires external intelligence gathering. (See "Building Intelligence Resources" in Chapter 9.)
5. Engaging in data mining or inferential data attacks on the target's databases. The database may be a commercial, publicly available one. Or, it could be one that is completely proprietary: for internal use only. Either way, an intelligence analyst or a spy will get access to it if possible. Using SQL, Structured Query Language, they can mine the database for the desired data. We'll discuss SQL more in-depth near the end of this chapter.

FRANCIS BACON, PROPHET OF ECONOMIC INTELLIGENCE GATHERING

Francis Bacon in the early seventeenth century coined the phrase: "Knowledge is Power." This English philosopher and writer envisioned the whole knowledge industry that has come to be accepted as part of our modern world. In 1620, he wrote *Novum Organon,* a guide for new ways of discovering knowledge. He recognized inductive reasoning as a tool for sifting through "facts."

Prior to Bacon, deductive logic dominated Western thought. Deductive logic goes from general principles to specific conclusions. Based upon Aristotle's syllogism, which hold that if A=B and C=A, then C=B, the technique is useful for testing existing truths. The example is "All men are animals. Socrates is a man. Therefore, Socrates is an animal." If the premises are true, the conclusion has to be true, provided the rules of logic are followed. The problem with deductive logic is that it makes discovering new knowledge a bit of a challenge, if not very difficult.

In inductive logic, one starts with the specific and goes to the general principle. The specific can be a series of observations. If one has enough facts or information, drawing a general principle is possible. But, the danger becomes that the conclusion does not always absolutely follow from the observations or facts. Yet, inductive logic is the basis of all intelligence gathering: trying to put bits and pieces together in a puzzle solution that makes sense.

Bacon's *New Atlantis* (published in 1625) conceives of a society constantly on the offensive in gathering knowledge. At the center of this activity is Saloman's House. The house periodically sends agents abroad in disguise. These agents report scientific discoveries. They provide "Knowledge of the affairs and state" of various countries. The "Merchants of Light" search all published material for the New Atlantis. Collecting information of all mechanical devices, the "Mystery Men" turn the information over to analysts known as the "Compilers." Based upon the analysts' work product, the men of action or "appliers," known as the Dowry Men or Benefactors, implement the knowledge into New Atlantis.

Bacon's writings define modern business intelligence. They also prophetically describe the organization and actions of countries like China, Japan, France, and Russia. All of them have had, or still do have, directorates or ministries for gathering economic intelligence. The lesson from Bacon is a lot of people are out there on the offensive doing industrial espionage. Modern security practice should dictate that a strong offensive intelligence program counterbalances IE efforts. Think of physical security as an exercise in deductive logic. It can do a good job in protecting against known threats. Then, consider intelligence gathering as an exercise in inductive logic. It aids in identifying new threats. Both approaches, used together, may harden a company against industrial espionage.

SQL AND DATA MINING

Data mining is a big business. Companies are drowning in data, so they hire firms specializing in analytics, who sift through mountains of factoids to create knowledge. We are not talking about data mining in this commercial sense.

Rather, we are looking at what an industrial spy could do with a database. A spy mines the database with very specific intent. The database may be proprietary; in that case, the spy devises a plan to gain access. After gaining access, the spy could use SQL to do searches for the needed data. (More about SQL in a minute.) The target's data, if publicly available, may generate the database for commercial release. Databases issued by third party vendors or governmental agencies may also hold valuable information. These open source databases may have their own search engines. Or, interrogating them using SQL may be an option.

Regardless of the source, normally constructed like a table, a database follows a row and column format. The database's fields form the columns with the individual records creating the horizontal rows. For example, a database of the books in my library would have the fields: "Title," "Author," "Publisher," "Subject," and "Year Published." Each individual book serves as the individual record or row. SQL, a language based upon English, enables me to search the database. An SQL statement interrogates the database as follows:

Select * from BOOKS_TABLE where YEAR_PUB = 1966

The statements says in everyday English: "select all records (* means "all") from the Books database where the year of publication equals 1966."

Now let's look at a practical problem where an industrial spy may use SQL to derive information from a database. Electrical Filters International developed a new electrical filtering device, the VFS138, used with UPS units (uninterruptible power sources) to attenuate power spikes to safe levels. The device has great potential in protecting computer systems. Unfortunately, the company, as of yet, has not sold the device to the general business community. So, the spy's client is having a hard time getting its hands on a unit. What the client wants the spy to obtain is a list of those businesses receiving a trial installation in the last six months.

In researching the problem, the spy learns he cannot develop a source at the target to gain access to the proprietary database within the client's deadline. However, the spy does have a source at a computer manufacturer that has collected information on the electrical spike problem from its customers. The spy's source checks the database and reports that it identifies various filtering devices by product name and the customer's name and address. So, the spy has the source run this query:

Select CUST_NAME, CUST_ADDR from FILTER_TABLE where FILTER = 'VFS138' and INSTALL_DATE between to_date('01-JAN-2002) and to_date('30-JUN-2002')

First, case is not critical in most implementations of SQL. In our example, we made the field names and the table name in upper case so they will stand out. The commands and functions are in lower case. If we reversed the case or mixed the case, it would have no effect on SQL being able read the inquiry. In everyday English, the query says, "Select from the FILTER database the customer's name and address where the electrical filter is the VFS138, and it has been installed between Jan. 1, 2002 and June 30, 2002." Most field names (column headings) in SQL are one word like FILTER, or if they are more than one word long like CUST_NAME, then the underscore character links the words together. The functions "between" and the auxiliary "to_date" enable the date range search.

The aim here is not to make the reader an expert on SQL. (However, familiarity with SQL is not that difficult to acquire. And, any twenty-first century security specialist would benefit from learning the concepts behind SQL. If you don't learn anything else about computing languages, learn SQL. Its logic and linguistic manipulations offer understanding and insight on what goes on behind the scenes in computer programming. Everyone uses databases, so don't be ignorant about how to get information from them.) Instead, we seek to show that databases are vulnerable. Someone always has access to the one sought after. And, that person can serve as a source to a spy. Also, with the endless ways information changes hands today, if a spy can't attack the target directly, they can find secondary source like a vendor or supplier that has the data. The conflict between the need for information in commerce and the desire for secrecy will continue to plague security in the twenty-first century.

DISCUSSION

As an exercise in using knowledge as an intelligence tool, try the following with open sources:

1. Pick up an employment or job news weekly at the supermarket or at the newsstand. Review the employment ads carefully, looking for clues about what directions the employer may be going in growth and development. Call the telephone number given in the ad. Ask about the number of people they are hiring and what other jobs are open. Push the envelope a bit and see what details regarding the company's research programs they will discuss over the telephone. If a Web site is available, see what you can learn there about the company's research efforts.

2. Choose a major employer in your area. Develop a timeline for the last five years of when they have hired employees in significant numbers and when they have laid people off. Be sure to document the numbers involved and the sources that you use.

3. Locate the names, current employers, and titles of three leading scientists in the biotechnology field. Develop a three-page biographical summary on one of them. Cite your sources.

4. Locate an expert in two of the following areas: (a) Fractures in steel on bridges, (b) Computer architecture design, (c) Fuzzy logic, (d) Bioterrorism, or (e) Developing vaccines against tuberculosis. Cite your sources and describe the search strategy you used for each.

5. Investigate whether you could develop an electronic backdoor into a company through one of its vendors. Develop a scenario for how you would use employment at the vendor as a cover. Or, devise a plan on how you would use weaknesses in the vendor's IT (information technology) system to penetrate their client.

(Please keep this as a theoretical exercise, no hacking or other illegal activity.) Document any research sources you use.

6. For one of the experts identified in Exercise Four above, locate testimony by that expert before a governmental agency. Or, find a paper given before a technical or scientific society. What facts do you glean about the expert's research from the record? Document the sources found and how you located the information.

7. Find two journals that regularly carry articles on the genetics of corn. From those journals, determine a major research center on corn genetics.

FOR FURTHER READING

1. Ben Forta, *SAMS Teach Yourself SQL in 10 Minutes,* SAMS, 2000.

2. W. Bradford Ashton, Richard A. Klavani, editors, *Keeping Abreast of Science and Technology: Technical Intelligence for Business,* Battelle Press, 1997.

3. John Michael Archer, *Sovereignty and Intelligence: Spying and Court Culture in the English Renaissance,* Stanford University Press, 1993. Provides a good overview of the ideas of Francis Bacon regarding intelligence gathering.

Chapter 3

BEGINNINGS IN ENGLAND

Since the text seeks to show how industrial espionage techniques developed over centuries, the Elizabethan Age is an apt starting point. The "birth" of spying in the West happened in this robust era, where the distinction between the man of letters and the purveyor of intrigue blurred in remarkable personalities. Elizabethan spies left an interesting legacy. Tales abound concerning secret codes and dark plots behind the Virgin Queen's throne. Elizabeth I was a clever, remarkable politician who understood she needed information in order to survive in power. If we dismiss the questionable stories about secret codes or hidden messages in Shakespeare's plays, we still uncover an exciting period of spying, filled with craft in use even today.

Francis Walsingham, an intellectual who understood European politics and affairs better than most of his countrymen, served Elizabeth's intelligence needs remarkably well. As the spymaster, he organized the first systematic, efficient secret service. Winston Churchill in his *A History of the English-Speaking Peoples: The New World* observes that Walsingham's intelligence service was effective in tracking down Spanish spies and English traitors. Elizabeth's England had two primary enemies: Spain and English Catholics. Spain was rich with treasures from the New World. In possession of a large seagoing navy, not just a coastal fleet, the Spain monarchy sought maritime domination of Europe and was covetous of English influence, while the island remained in the embrace of Protestantism. English Catholics held stiff opposition to Elizabeth's affirmation of the Protestant faith.

Walsingham's genius lay in his ability to recognize information essential to political power resides at several levels. Unlike today's CIA, the former KGB, or Israel's Mossad, Elizabethan espionage was not a highly organized, centralized civil service bureaucracy. Rather, the intelligence apparatus was in the hands of court aristocrats like Walsingham. Built upon patronage, Walsingham's service employed associates to act as operatives both in England and abroad. It was a network of informants, couriers, diplomats, and salaried spies stretching across Europe from Calais to Istanbul. These agents, encouraged to draw intelligence from various levels of society, talked to merchants, soldiers, naval personnel, dock workers, brokers, diplomats, and financiers.

Although intelligence gathering in the period resembled more like today's newspaper reporting, it represented a giant step forward. Walsingham realized that a modern state required more than court gossip to be successful. None of the modern information sources that we take for granted existed. No newspapers, magazines, or journals were available from the local market or the apothecary. In the transformation from a medieval kingdom to a world power, England's Walsingham understood that gathering information from people-in-the-know formed a pillar for the modern state. Walsingham then, at least in the Anglo-American sphere, became the father of human intelligence gathering (HUMINT in intelligence lingo). The person having inside information remains today as one of the most sought-after intelligence resources.

What then were the skills of the Elizabethan spy? The Renaissance spy needed enough education to converse with men from all walks of life, the cultivated gentleman and the uncultivated laborer. Knowledge of various languages was also helpful, especially if working on the Continent. He also required the power of observation, a good memory, and the ability to draw diagrams of fortifications or manufacturing works later after seeing them hours or days prior. But most important, the Elizabethan spy had to accept a new code of ethics. Serving the state became paramount; missions could not be clouded with personal concerns or feelings. Personal ethics, as Niccolo Machiavelli observed in *The Prince,* became subservient to the needs of the state.

What one would not do in one's personal life emerged as being acceptable when acting for Queen and country. The modern industrial spy may not heed even this ethos. While some act for country, many seek only financial gain. Regardless of their motives, expect no quarter or compassion. Outdoing an opponent with treachery, that is the inheritance of Walsingham; spying remains the most heartless of professions.

Christopher Marlowe, the famous Elizabethan poet and playwright, was an ideal spy for Walsingham's service. Well educated, he knew the universal language of Europe, Latin, and some French and Italian to make his passage in Continental circles reasonably smooth. Thanks to the intervention of the Queen's Privy Council, he received an M.A. degree from Cambridge University in 1587. Cambridge faculty members had reservations about awarding him the degree due to accusations of him leaning toward the Catholic cause. His detractors heard stories about him going to Rheims on the Continent, a center for English Catholic scholars and discontents.

Actually, Marlowe almost fell victim to his own disinformation or cover story. He operated primarily in the Low Countries (The Netherlands and Belgium) gathering intelligence for Walsingham while pretending to be a Catholic sympathizer. Keeping the company of students, poets, scientists, and other spies, he passed on to the Crown's spymaster reports on commerce, politics, military matters, and Papist plotting. Marlowe's guise constituted a false flag recruitment of Catholic enemies of the Queen. He pretended to be one of them to learn what they had to say. A technique still very much with us in the twenty-first century, the false flag still allows modern industrial spies to befriend a company's malcontents to penetrate its secrets.

Recruited in 1585, the year of the war in The Netherlands, Marlowe was able to earn more as a spy than as an academic or a writer thanks to the £2000 made available to Walsingham's service for intelligence operations. His knowledge of language, and its attendant devotion to detail, was necessary for utilizing the codes and ciphers required by the times. Charles Nicholl in *The Reckoning* (Harcourt Brace & Company, 1992) notes that intelligence in Marlowe's time moved at the speed of a rider on horseback. Interception of reports and messages was a very real possibility. Ciphering emerged as a vital skill for spies. Most likely, Marlowe carried a copy of the standard code and cipher reference for the period, della Porta's *De Furtivis Literarum Notis*. Cryptography continues to play a role in the realm of industrial espionage. Breaking ciphers is an essential part of the commercial spy's bag of tricks. Like in Marlowe's time, secrets still fall to interception and compromise.

The spying game influenced Marlowe's work. *Tamburlaine*, his play written in 1587, includes a speech about fortifying a garrison. The language is a paraphrase of passage from another English spy's technical manual, *The Practice of Fortification* by Paul Ive, which was published in

1589. Marlowe represents the prototype of the modern spy, an educated, careful observer.

What was missing from Elizabethan intelligence was a systematic method for evaluating information. The intelligence lacked refinement. It didn't have a sifting process to separate opinion, gossip, and speculation from facts. Marlowe did not have a regular newspaper or magazine at his disposal, never mind the Internet or electronic databases. Crosschecking against other sources of information was difficult to accomplish. Rating sources for validity and for reliability was not a part of the intelligence process. The intelligence end product differed little from the raw intelligence the field agent gathered. Often the raw data received no intelligence analysis.

His recognized literary triumph, *The Tragical History of Doctor Faustus,* tells the story of a learned man who bargains with the Dark Prince to achieve worldly power and wealth at the cost of his soul. Marlowe certainly dealt with the dark side of human nature while in the English secret service. Lying and misrepresentation were the tools of his trade. Despite his return to the literary world, he died a young man in 1593 at a Deptford lodging house, the victim of a stabbing in a tavern brawl. Whether his death stemmed from his spying activities remains a subject of literary and historical debate. What does appear true though is that spies can be some of the brightest people, capable of great perfidy and the Faustian bargain. Underestimating their creativity, cunning, and resourcefulness exposes your company's intellectual capital to plunder.

BRITISH INDUSTRIALISM IN THE EIGHTEENTH AND NINETEENTH CENTURIES

From the time of Elizabeth through the nineteenth century, Britain grew from a backward medieval realm rife with civil conflicts to a stable, great industrial power. Part of this ascendance was a product of intelligence gathering. Ideas and information flowed into Britain. By jumping into the industrial revolution, England entered a growing world of commerce in goods and in innovation. Britain became both a magnet and a source for intellectual capital. Churchill remarks in his *History: The Age of Revolution* that the monopoly of the landed classes on the economy, social structure, and culture came to an end. The rise of free markets precluded the medieval oligarchy.

Societies ruled by elite classes, if competent and knowledgeable, control information and its dissemination quite well. Only the select few acquire access to learning and the power that knowledge affords. Building castles around centers of learning and information was feasible and desirable. When Britain, and subsequently America, transformed from agrarian to industrial economies they welcomed free markets both in trade and in ideas.

Churchill comments that in America a conflict arose between Thomas Jefferson and Alexander Hamilton on whether America would remain primarily agricultural or become industrialized. Jefferson feared the consequences of a mass industrial society. Democracy was fine for a cultivated, enlightened ruling body of men, but the masses of workers running society could produce chaos. Jefferson, far from advocating oppression, felt that commerce needed to stay within certain bounds to protect the safety of the republic.

Hamilton by contrast saw America's future in industrial development and commerce. He judged that by following the path of Britain, the result would be a prosperous American nation linked to the commerce of the world. The decision of the English-speaking nations to move toward free markets, to partake of Hamilton's vision, had a profound impact on world history. In the late twentieth century the former Soviet Union and Eastern Europe finally had to confront this choice. These centrally controlled oligarchies could no longer function in a world of free markets, for the technology of mass digital communication made their isolation a madman's delusion.

The Berlin Wall tumbled. Despite the euphoria of that moment, a new warfare emerged. Open societies became prey not only for military and political secrets but also for economic espionage. The stealing and pirating of intellectual capital grew on a whole new scale. Motivated by competition and greed, some states developed an intelligence elite composed of well-educated men and women like a Christopher Marlowe in the sixteenth century. They visit the world's centers of innovation like the agents in Francis Bacon's *The New Atlantis*. And, they look and gather, observing and absorbing the ideas of others.

In the eighteenth century, British textiles, hardware, steel, coke-iron, steam power, and glass industries all came under prying eyes. When a nation is successful in producing a good, a product, or a service, other countries want to partake of that success. The ethical fulfillment of this desire is to license the technology to other countries or competitors. By this process humanity at large benefits from new discoveries with the innovators receiving a fair return on their investment. But if reasoned, enlightened action prevailed in the world, war and cruelty probably would be absent. As Machiavelli counsels in *The Prince,* we must see men and women as they are, not as we wish them to be. The reality is that we live in the midst of an information war, a free-for-all battle for a precious commodity: knowledge.

Looking at the eighteenth century glass industry will further establish that "borrowing" technology has been with us for centuries. Glass with its translucence and strength has made our lives easier and certainly brighter. The technology of glassmaking carries a broad impact across a wide spectrum of industries: architectural materials, automobiles, and aircraft all come to mind. Our industrial ancestors in England and France saw similar applications within the industries of their time. The common method of plate glass manufacture in England was broad sheet. A glass worker gathers molten glass on a blowpipe, and blows it into a balloon shape. Then, the worker cuts the ends off and splits the remaining hot glass cylinder with a pair of shears. Flattened on an iron plate, the molten cylinder becomes a plate of glass. The problem with this method was that the resulting glass had a wavy appearance. If you see this type of plate glass in existing American Colonial homes, the distortion is quite apparent.

The French developed a method of casting plate glass producing less distortion. From 1773 to the 1790s, the British copied French casting methods. And, of course, the technology made its way to America. But the glass wars didn't end with plate glass. The English excelled at bottle manufacture. Glass bottle making was going strong in England in the seventeenth century. In fact, the first glass bottle manufacturing plant in America was in Jamestown, Virginia in the early 1600s. The French borrowed English bottle making methods resulting in a cross-transfer of glass technology.

Glass technology passed from one country to another via several paths. Workers, merchants, tradesmen, teamsters, and longshoremen traded observations on what they saw in daily business. Owners or operators visited factories in England and in France. Customers and vendors spoke of what they knew about the processes. And of course, industrial spying played a role when osmosis through commercial contact didn't fill in all the details. The need for commerce worked against the need for secrecy. Protecting trade secrets, as the transfer of glass technology shows, remains a tightrope walk without a safety net. The knowledge has to be disseminated to a limited degree, but not too much, or the owner loses the legal and *de facto* rights to the trade secret. (See Chapter 10 for more on trade secrets.)

Unfortunately, these outflows of technology were a problem Britain and the other European manufacturing powers could not fully address. As indicated earlier in Chapter One, Francis Cabot Lowell from 1811-1813 studied the British textile industry. This calculated industrial espionage brought the Cartwright loom to America.

Andrew Carnegie, who built the steel industry in America, commented that he could not have created the steel industry alone. He relied upon technical intelligence he gathered in Europe. America grew into the "Guilded Age" of the late nineteenth century with borrowed and purloined intellectual capital. Perhaps, this information challenges the self-reliant image of our national identity. But, ignoring realities doesn't help us understand the enterprise known as industrial espionage. Realize that America rose as an industrial power from its colonial beginnings up to the time of the Second World War by shopping the world for ideas. But, also be aware that since 1945, according to John J. Fialka in *War by Other Means,* other countries started coming to us to acquire our knowledge. We have ceased being an intellectual debtor nation to that of a creditor (without hope of repayment). This fact promises to keep security professionals busy well into the twenty-first century.

OTHER LESSONS

Spying is probably the oddest of professions. When doing it for one's country, espionage becomes acceptable at least at the ethical margins. The process still involves thievery and brutal manipulation of others, but we accept the trade's dark side as a means to national survival. When the trade brings its baggage to the private sector, we become morally appalled, and we are right in feeling this way. Industrial espionage is a mean, nasty business by any definition.

But, intelligence gathering does possess an intellectual side. After all, it attracted a genius like Marlowe. With an emphasis on analyzing data and making inferences, the intelligence game can be an interesting challenge for the mind. Outwitting an opponent is another allure. Initially, the game may beckon us to espionage's dark techniques. Tempting us to become as wanton as the spies, counterespionage methods dictate restraint if we are not to become like the perpetrators we chase. We must enjoy the game, but not too much.

Having some principles is essential to our mission. Trampling upon the rights of other people simply will not do, no matter how lofty the motives. Frequently, the security professional may be without allies in trying to remain in the morally responsible zone. A stark loneliness exists there without a king, queen, or country to be fighting for. The corporation is impersonal, and it lacks a flag to rally around. Devoting one's life to a company, oh well, that lifestyle choice that deserves some very careful self-assessment to say the least.

What we are fighting for is to protect the livelihoods of the rank and file people that depend on the company, who work hard to support their families. If our clients lose their intellectual assets, they can go out of business precipitously. By protecting an impersonal corporation, we are fighting for our coworkers, people who have bills to pay. They deserve fair treatment, vigilance on our part, and dedication to fighting industrial espionage in a legal, just way.

Intelligence, responsibly collected, will be the key to protecting the twenty-first century business against information predators. In security, we have to move from behind static defenses and from passive observation to active information gathering. We must open new eyes and new ears. Renaissance England explored the world and made Britain a world power. We need to ride on the same wave of spirit in the twenty-first century security game.

DISCUSSION

1. Spying in Marlowe's time resembled the news gathering activity of journalism since open sources largely did not exist. Instead of informing the public, the agents reported back to their handlers at court. The principals received their own personal news service

on what was going on in military, diplomatic, and commercial affairs. In our time, we are overwhelmed with open sources, especially electronic ones; data collection can be immediate and relatively inexpensive. The challenge is to sift out knowledge from an ocean of data.

How in-depth are electronic databases such as Web sites and commercial databases? What are the tests of reliability and validity in these sources? These issues are central to anyone collecting open source intelligence. In Marlowe's time any news was welcomed, because society was information poor. Today's spy must be more discriminating. In wading through too much information, today's overabundance, the intelligence gatherer must be able to divide the false from the true. This plethora of data can work to security's advantage though. We can use certain information to cloak or to screen sensitive operations. (See Chapter 4, the "Cloaking" section.)

As an exercise to what intelligence gatherers must go through, develop some standards for testing the reliability of open sources. In other words, how often is their information correct? How do you determine the track record for a source? Is there greater reliability for a printed open source as opposed to an electronic one?

Also, address the validity issue. How well does the source correspond to reality? What methods could you develop to test validity? What crosschecking measures would you have to employ to insure the validity of sources? Again, evaluate printed sources versus electronic sources in the light of validity.

2. A discussion of intelligence gathering's role in security will take place in Chapters 8 and 9. In anticipation, describe why reliability and validity tests are important concerns for the security specialist. How do they impact on doing counterintelligence?

3. In 1985, Michael Sekora, a physicist at the Defense Intelligence Agency, proposed a database to track the development and flow of key technologies around the globe. Perhaps it would be a digitizing of Francis Bacon's and Walsingham's ideas, acting as a clearinghouse on technology transfer. Given the name "Socrates," it was not established by the U.S. government. However, nothing prevents using private commercial databases to accomplish the same end. What information resources could you use to monitor technology transfer in your company's industry?

(Hint: The sources discussed in Chapter 2 would be a good starting point. *Online* magazine, a bimonthly review of electronic databases for information professionals, is another good resource. The Web site is http://www.onlinemag.net.)

4. Christopher Marlowe had a classical education from Cambridge University. Skilled in languages, he was well equipped to be a spy in the sixteenth century. What background should a modern industrial spy possess? What kind of training is necessary for the security specialist in combating industrial espionage? Latin was the universal language in the Elizabethan Age. Has a knowledge of a computer language like C, or a database language such as SQL, become a necessary universal requirement in the security field?

5. We discussed earlier technology transfers between England and France regarding glass manufacture. In our time, the personal computer was the product of two companies: IBM and Apple. Each company created its own approach and design. At first the differences between the machines were quite clear. The Macintosh had a graphic interface while the IBM machine began with a command line based upon MS.DOS. Eventually the two systems became more alike. The IBM clones adopted a graphical interface, and the Apple machines were able to process files from IBM disks. Discuss how technology transfer played a role in developing standards for the user interface.

6. Was Britain's decline as the major industrial power due to industrial espionage? If so, will a similar fate await America? At what point does our Gross Intellectual Product (GIP) fail to exceed outflows to other countries? Cite five American industries that have significantly declined or disappeared in the last 50 years.

FOR FURTHER READING

1. For more about Marlowe and Elizabethan spying consult Charles Nicholl's *The Reckoning* (Harcourt Brace & Company, 1992.)

2. *Online* magazine, published by Information Today, Medford, New Jersey, ISSN: 0146-5422.

3. For more historical information about the eighteenth century read J.R. Harris's *Industrial Espionage and Technology Transfer: Britain and France in the 18th Century,* (Ashgate, 1998).

Chapter 4

MORE OBSERVATION TECHNIQUES

In Chapter 1 we discussed observational techniques based upon sight: eyeballing the competition. With advances in technology, however, observation now goes beyond direct visual examination of a target. This chapter will cover aerial surveillance, computer research, satellite photography, and other methods.

Aerial surveillance as a serious intelligence tool began during the American Civil War. Union military forces employed aerial balloons as observation posts on Confederate troop movements and defenses. Used in the Peninsular Campaign by General George B. McClellan's troops in the attempt to take Richmond, Virginia in 1862, the balloons afforded a high ground perspective. This was an advantage on the flat, tidewater terrain of the James peninsula situated between the York and James rivers. Woodlands and natural vegetation, however, acted to camouflage trench defenses, fortifications, and troop deployments.

McClellan's inabilities to gauge accurately the enemy force's size lead to his ambivalence and his indecisive action in the campaign. He eventually withdrew from the battlefield. While new ways to look at the battlefield were emerging via aerial balloons, scientific interpretation was still in the future. Without reliable interpretation methods for aerial data, McClellan remained blind.

Interpretation recognizes that no human activity occurs in isolation. Erecting homes and buildings requires a means to bring construction materials and workers to the site. Activity by road or rail is visible from the air. The frequency of the traffic reveals the scale of the project. Just as the number of filled parking spaces indicates a plant's number of workers, the number of railcars on a siding tells something about the level of production. If the cars are open and contain say coal, sand, or iron ore, calculating the consumption of raw materials is not difficult. The same estimating process goes for trucks or delivery vans by noting the number and frequency of deliveries. At a concrete plant, for example, the height and width of aggregate piles indicate the level of production. Similar predictions are possible for barrels of chemicals or chemical railcars. All of this intelligence gathering can be done via aerial observation.

If a manufacturer builds motor homes, the number of furnace/AC units in the storage yard provides a clue on future production levels. Raw materials, composites, semi-finished goods on storage yard racks, forklifts, workers at various tasks, waste bins, and emissions all carry a Siren's song of activity to an eye in the sky. An analog in the military sector, aerial observers count supplies, troops, tanks, "humvees," aircraft, and ships. The technique remains constant whether the target is civil or military.

R.V. Jones in World War Two served as one of Churchill's scientific officers. He learned during the course of the war that photographs, especially from the air, lent to interpretation for military purposes. They were used to unravel Germany's secret weapon programs. The Allies employed photography to tell that a hydroelectric facility in Norway had the ability to manufacture "heavy water," deuterium oxide, a buffer to moderate nuclear reactions. Based upon the photographic intelligence, a commando raid destroyed the facility, which caused a profound disruption of the Nazis' nuclear program.

Aerial surveillance comes in several flavors, (1) viewing from a nearby building or a natural elevation, (2) using photography from an aircraft, (3) spying via an aerial balloon, kite, or drone, and (4) peering by a satellite from space. None of these methods are terribly complex or expensive. In many cases, someone else may have already taken the photos for the spy.

Aerial or satellite photographs for most of the United States are available from commercial and governmental sources. *The Investigator's Little Black Book 2* (Crime Time Publishing, 1998), a pocket reference for private investigators and business intelligence specialists, lists several sources under "Aerial & Satellite Photographs." The investigative and commercial intelligence communities definitely know about these resources. For up-to-the-minute photographs of a target's site, renting an aircraft or helicopter or even using a drone are possible. Adapted model aircraft, kites, and large balloons all serve as reliable drones.

Used in accident site investigations, nothing prevents their deployment in business intelligence gathering.

The best defense against aerial observation is cloaking. Obviously, some operations are of such large scale that cloaking would be difficult or too expensive. If your client operates an electric power generation plant, then hiding open boxcars of coal becomes a bit problematical. But, many high technology processes lend themselves to cloaking techniques. Keeping key materials and ingredients out sight may be feasible, provided safe, secure internal storage facilities exist.

Limits on cloaking methods exist only by the restrictions one places on the imagination. Recently a program on one of the Discovery® channels profiled freelance photographers for automotive magazines. They earn substantial fees by getting photographs of new models prior to their release to the public. Manufacturers test these new vehicles at secret tracks around the United States. Using long-range lenses, the freelancers shoot pictures of the vehicles during their test trials. Automobile manufactures now cloak their vehicles with inflatable vinyl "jackets" or aprons that cover the body of the vehicle below the windows. These jackets distort the true contours and characteristics of the vehicle's exterior design. This method represents a simple, but ingenious cloaking technique. We'll discuss other cloaking methods at the end of the chapter.

Aerial observation focuses on the following indicators, which tell a fairly complete story of what is going on at a plant:

1. *Use.* Wear on roads, railroad tracks, loading docks, and on parking areas. Ruts in dirt roads or on the shoulders of paved roads, skid or tire marks on pavement, excessive potholes on paved surfaces, shiny railroad tracks, and goods piled on docks are all signs of heavy use.

2. *Numbers.* Employees outside at lunch hours or at change of shift, delivery trucks, roads and rail lines serving the site, water towers or water reservoirs for fire protection or industrial processing, electrical lines and substations, buildings and support structures, above ground pipe and conduits,

3. *Amounts.* Equipment, raw materials, trash bins, and emissions. Taking photographs at different times of the day over a period of a couple of weeks will provide enough information to make estimates of the production flow through the site.

4. *Changes.* Buildings under construction or being torn down; relocations of equipment, materials and goods; roads, waterways, or railroad spurs under construction; additional power resources.

Up to this point, we've considered mainly observation of the physical plant from the sky. What about, however, businesses where the physical plant's layout does not say much to a bird in the sky? Companies that produce primarily data respond to a different type of observation. Software manufacturers, design companies, consulting firms, and media companies have electrons as their lifeblood. Penetrating their computer systems becomes necessary to find out what's going on inside.

COMPUTER SYSTEMS

In Clifford Stoll's *The Cuckoo's Egg* (Doubleday, 1989), the author, an astronomer tasked with maintaining the UNIX system at the Lawrence Berkeley Laboratory (LBL) in Berkeley, California discovered a maze of computer espionage stretching from Europe to America. The end papers' diagram traces Internet links between a hacker in Germany and the LBL in California, with the university and military nodes plotted along the way. A path winding through computer systems at the University of Bremen, a defense contractor in McLean, Virginia and the Jet Propulsion Laboratory in Pasadena uncovers a disturbing truth. Information thieves do not have to scale your castle's walls or assault the portcullis, after crossing the moat that you dug with care. They do not have to follow your preconceived battle plan. Multiple paths exist to your sensitive files and secrets. They can seek an inside track on the electronic highway.

Information systems rely on complexity. With increasing complexity, the vectors for attack become latent and labyrinthine. Stoll saw the future. He sounded the alarm that computer security had inherent insecurity. His book has relevance today and remains in print over a decade later in a world where computer books drop out of sight at a maddening pace.

Despite all the buzzwords like "firewall," "intrusion detection," "proxy server," "security logs," and "DMZ," computer networks encounter penetrations all the time. Despite all the magazines, certification programs, news stories, and even television specials surrounding computer security, the crimes keep coming and growing. Why do system compromises continue? Why are we still on the bucket brigade for the Titanic? We keep bailing, but barely manage to stay afloat.

Stoll's methods for resolving the system attacks supply some answers on keeping the ship above the waterline. First, as a scientist, he approached the electronic infiltration as a puzzle begging for a solution. He sought to understand the intruder. While some of his colleagues were contented simply to knock the hacker off their systems, he wanted to know when the attacks occurred and where the intruder wanted to go on the UNIX system. Once he learned the spy's *modus operandi,* his M.O., then he could craft a plan to trap the offender.

In the course of studying the spy, Stoll acquired the telecommunications path that permitted the intruder's access to the LBL. He discovered the flaw in the operating system that provided a weakness in the security defenses sufficient for the Internet spy to gain entry. But most important, he realized the spy's thirst for military-related technology was unquenchable. That perception led to the data bandit's demise in cyberspace. Sharing this information with law enforcement insured the eventual tracing of the hacker's location to Germany. Measuring the duration of the attacks helped Stoll realize that a delaying tactic was necessary if the perpetrator was to stay online long enough to permit the tracing. Otherwise, the sessions on the LBL system would have been too brief.

Since he knew the spy was interested in military applications, Stoll pulled off the ultimate fakery. He created folders (directories) filled with pseudotechnical documents. On face value, they spun technical tales with a certain military flavor. Actually an amalgamation of techno-babble, they took a long time to peruse, and that is all Stoll needed. Downloading times also helped to lengthen the session times. Stoll's course of action has become a hallmark of innovative security thinking. He employed deception as weapon against a foe, rather than just remain a victim of it. And, he took time to learn his opponent's intent and methods.

His almost playful, inquisitive approach combined humility and creativity. He was humble enough to accept maybe that an opponent could teach him something. But, he possessed enough pliable creativity to foist a clever deception on a wily hacker. With this method, he had a major role in bringing down spies trying to gather military secrets to sell to the Soviet Union.

Spies infiltrating via the electronic highway are not disappearing. Put your finger on the defense, and they'll find passage around it. Or, they'll locate someone who will let them in. Their tactics vary from deception to bribery to blackmail, depending on the person they need to compromise.

Peter Heims in *Countering Industrial Espionage* (20th Century Security Education, 1982) identified multiple avenues of penetration or compromise for computer systems. He recognized that unauthorized observation of data could occur at any point in the information processing cycle. Created at the height of the main frame era, Heim's insights still hold relevance today. While the focus of business computing has moved from centralized processing to networking, and increasingly, to mobile computing, the threat points remain the same. Those points of vulnerability to watch are:

A. Technology or Process
　　1. *Interception of communications:* terminal, telephone line, or telephone junction box.
　　2. *At the monitor:* photographing or printing the screen, piggybacking (using someone else's monitor or terminal while they are away but are still logged in), and unauthorized access (using another's password and login).
　　3. *Disk Drives:* diskettes copied, or stolen and files erased (sabotage).
　　4. *Magnetic Tape Drives:* copied or stolen or tapes erased; substituted with erroneous data on the tape (another form of sabotage).
　　5. *Printers:* extra unauthorized copies of reports and documents printed. Confidential documents seen by unauthorized eyes at printer, and documents photocopied or photographed.
　6. *Waste:* paper captured from the trash, computer media retrieved and read, and "obsolete" computers having their hard drives read.
B. People
　　1. *Clerical:* steal data, alter or forge data.
　　2. *Computer Operators and Users:* copy files, sabotaging of data.
　　3. *Programmers:* theft of proprietary software or data, unauthorized altering of programming code.

Heims also recognizes that sabotage fits into the industrial espionage equation too. A competitor may not always be in the economic position to exploit stolen intellectual property. The risks always exist that a theft could be linked to them. Sabotage or distortion of a competitor's mission-critical information, if cleverly done, creates immense havoc for the target. Deleting the accounts receivable database is Hurricane Andrew and a West Coast earthquake rolled into one for the target. Distorting or corrupting information on the credit database may grant terms to bad risks. Sabotage has dire consequences in the information sector. When your client spends money on information security, they are also protecting against that threat too. At budget time for security, make sure the management team understands that concept.

Needless to say further, unauthorized observation of your business' electronic information remains one of the worst scenarios. Combining effective Information Technology/Network security measures (something we'll discuss in Chapter 7) with creativity and strategic thinking (like Stoll demonstrated) affords considerable protection. Yet, these measures are far from static, one-time solutions. Constant auditing of accounts on your system and surveillance of user activity provide continuous protection. Fixed defenses can do a good job, as long as the security administrator's shadow constantly roams the network.

What will a spy look for when penetrating your IT security? A spy's checklist would include:

1. Personal information about high-level users. This data may lead to cracking passwords since users tend to create passwords derived from their daily lives. (See Chapter 5 for a detailed discussion.)
2. Access rights to computers or servers used by key personnel.
3. Raid the trash for computer printouts and tossed media like floppies.
4. Find hiding places in user's desks for passwords, floppies containing sensitive data, and notebooks (of the paper kind) containing logins and passwords.
5. Gain computer information via indirect methods. Can computer screens be seen from the street using high-powered binoculars? Or, can the spy pick up electronic emanations or computer wireless transmissions from a nearby observation post?

None of these techniques require the mastery of erudite hacking methods employing "buffer overflows" or "smashing the stack." But, they still can be quite effective. As a security specialist, possible countermeasures you could implement include:

1. Place password generation controls into your security program. They can prevent short passwords based upon personal information.

2. Enforce lockup procedures for computer media containing sensitive files when not in use. Train employees in how to reduce computer notebook theft. Make employees aware that a vendor, a housekeeper, a janitor, or a new acquaintance could be a spy. Point out that leaving sensitive material out and unattended only makes life easy for information thieves.

3. Make sure employees know how to use correctly any encryption software provided.

4. Tell employees that what they consider to be good hiding places rarely work. Inquisitive minds do find sticky notes under the desktop or in the book in the corner. If keeping track of multiple passwords becomes too tiresome, then suggest placing them in an encrypted electronic file. The file's pass phrase will be long enough to make it hard to crack. Preferably, the phrase should be something easy to remember, but difficult to guess. "Spies do not wear purple eyeglasses" is arbitrary, and a bit silly, but it is easy to remember and long enough to resist brute force attacks.

5. Install appropriate window shades or screens to prevent viewing monitors from the street. Have an electronics countermeasures expert measure the size of the emanations shadow cast by your terminals and monitors or by computer wireless operations. Install any shielding recommended by your expert.

MOBILE COMPUTING

We live in a world where people want to be connected 24 hours per today. This fact, of course, offers convenience and access to information unparalleled in human history. Wireless technology continues to grow, increasing the dangers of interception. A work environment without borders means one without a security perimeter in the traditional sense.

Factors of protection need to be able to function in this mobile work arena. The first step in protection is tracking capability. If someone steals a computer notebook, a laptop, a palm-sized device, or a pocket computer, that device should have tracking software installed on the hard drive or in memory. This software will send a signal to a monitoring facility anytime someone connects to the Internet using the machine. The thief will not be able to detect the software, and it cannot be removed from the machine by a simple reformatting of the hard drive. This ability to track the device via the Internet assists law enforcement in recovering the machine. It also builds an electronic trail documenting where the thief logs onto the Internet.

Strong encryption tools need to be available to mobile computing users. We are not talking about off-the-shelf encryption software for $15.95 at the local computer store. And most definitely, we are not suggesting that any user rely on the standard password protection utilities or file encryption tools built into many word processing programs. Most of these tools afford little protection against someone who has even a small amount of cryptography knowledge. Stick to strong and tested cryptography algorithms such as PGP and Blowfish.

Using open source encryption like Blowfish, a 448-bit algorithm, is essential. With the algorithm being made public, leading cryptography experts get to test it and insure that it is not inherently flawed. Any software package that incorporates a strong algorithm should be transparent to the user. Users should not have to take any specific action to encrypt files once security installs the software. It will happen automatically; the user cannot forget anything. Another desirable feature is binary file shredding of deleted files and temporary files created by the operating system. Proper electronic shredding will prevent a thief from constructing the data from secondary or disposed files. For ultimate security, consider software that encrypts the entire hard drive rather than just files. This measure prevents a spy or thief from gaining access to the operating system, which could serve as a base for attack on the encrypted files. Please note though that some export and import restrictions may apply to encryption software taken to foreign countries.

The best algorithms will do little good if employees are not careful about leaving their portable computing devices unattended and turned off when not in use. And, if passwords or pass phrases are necessary, not guarding them with great care is sheer foolishness. If the user employs a VPN to communicate with the home office, he or she needs to follow all the security procedures for that VPN product. (Virtual Private Networks allow secure, encrypted transmissions across the Internet.) Again, staying logged in and unattended renders the best VPN useless. Field workers must employ the same secure waste disposal and trash procedures for computer media and for computer-generated paper as used in the office. If necessary, they should have high-grade portable shredders. (See "Trash Raiding" later in this chapter and the discussion of computers and computer media disposal in Chapter 7.)

In computer wireless networking, make sure your IT security staff stays current on the latest developments in the IEEE 802.11b standard with 128-bit encryption. As this technology grows in influence, the technical staff needs to stay on top of alerts, bulletins, and upgrades. Doing away with cabling saves money and greatly increases convenience, just make sure that your company is not providing an open channel for the rest of the world to listen in on your business. While this book aims at the security generalist, we do recommend the reader review an article on tips for securing wireless networking at http://www.extremetech.com/article2/0,3973,11400,00.asp. The material is fairly technical, so we are not going to go into the details here. But, the security generalist should keep up on the basic concepts of wireless technology to be able to have discussions with the IT staff and insure general oversight. Sources of information and ongoing intelligence on mobile and wireless computing are these magazines:

Mobile Computing
Handheld PC
HP Palmtop Paper
Mobile Computing and Communications
PC Laptop
Pen Computing
Portable Computing
Portable Design

The security professional should also consider holding periodic brainstorming sessions with the IT staff and with mobile computing users. These sessions can be forums for discussing and trading security ideas. They afford security the opportunity to see other points of views on the technology. Users and members of the technical staff become acquainted with security's concerns. (See Chapter 5, "Brainstorming" for more on the topic.)

ELECTRONIC EAVESDROPPING

Spying by intercepting electronic communication began with someone tapping into a telegraph line. Electronic snoops have been with us ever since those days. In 1972 when Russia was trying to negotiate rates on purchasing American grain, Russian intelligence monitored microwave transmissions. They listened in on telephone calls between United States traders and the United States Department of Agriculture. The monitoring gave the Russians an edge in leveraging bargain rates for grain.

The Russians continued monitoring American cellular telephone traffic by capturing satellite down links in the 1990s. This intelligence gathering originated from their satellite monitoring station in Lourdes, Cuba. American executives traveling to Europe and Asia in recent years became the targets of electronic surveillance. The French and the Chinese have been accused of bugging hotel rooms and even passenger seats on commercial aircraft.

Of course, allegations of wiretapping and electronic eavesdropping continue to occur domestically at all levels of American industry. The guiding rule of thumb becomes that assuming what you say on the telephone or even in a meeting will remain "secret" borders on being naïve.

This insidious observation technique isn't disappearing anytime soon. In most facilities, it is simply too easy to get away with undetected. Many businesses respond with panic countermeasures when they discover a "bug." Otherwise, they do not have an organized prevention plan in place. They do not allocate resources for this purpose, because they feel electronic eavesdropping will not happen in *their* company. As the cliché goes, "gentlemen do not read other gentlemen's mail." Unfortunately, few gentlemen or ladies exist in the industrial espionage game. Extremely miniaturized commercial surveillance equipment for both audio and video is available for sale on the Internet at reasonable cost. (Just check out "spy equipment" using an Internet search engine if you have any doubts.) People are not buying this gear for decoration. Anyone can get into the electronic spying business: an employee, a competitor, a snooping stockholder, a political activist doing the "watchdog thing" on your company, or an unethical journalist. For those that do not wish to purchase commercial equipment, parts and kits for bugging devices are available through electronics stores and catalogs.

Building equipment to monitor electronic emanations from digital equipment like monitors is feasible for those with a fundamental understanding of electronics. Again, such information is available on the Internet. If your client has valuable information, trust that someone will be trying to listen in on it or tap into the company's transmissions.

Without a rational, systematic electronic countermeasures program, the fear, upon the discovery of bugging, engenders paranoia even in normally stable businesses. The steps toward electromagnetic security should include:

- Assess your client's real vulnerabilities. If a spy does intercept your telecommunications, wireless cellular and network traffic, or digital emanations, what is the worst that will happen?
- Consider how much your client is "in play" as far as potential industrial espionage goes. Do your client's products and services offer a prime target? Is your client in an industry that has large-scale industrial espionage activity? (This evaluation will require external intelligence gathering, which we will discuss in Chapter 9.)
- If the risks are unacceptable, which means intercepts could cause grave harm, then institute a countermeasures program. Start with the basics: encrypt computer traffic wherever feasible and perform good physical security on in-house telecommunications facilities. Make sure all telephone and utility closets are locked down when not in use. And, when vendors enter these areas, insure that they have an escort. Have security patrols regularly check these areas to make sure they remained locked. The same procedures apply to server and network hub rooms.
- If you suspect someone is planting bugs or is doing a digital emanation capture, call in professional help. Common places for bugs include inside telephones, inside wall outlets, or under desks. Favorite places for taps include telecommunications closets, network hub rooms, and utility closets. Signs of digital emanation capture include suspicious vans parked near your facility or monitoring equipment found on your property. When in doubt, bring in some qualified assistance.

- An electronic countermeasures professional should have extensive background and training from the military or law enforcement. Plus, he or she should possess a Bachelor of Science or an M.S. degree in electronic or electrical engineering. Always obtain references from the expert on other corporate clients.

In addition to addressing any specific compromise of your electronic traffic, a qualified expert can assist in developing a plan to augment your existing electronic countermeasures. For example, after measuring your digital emanations shadow, the expert may recommend shielding parts of the computer system and erecting physical barriers, such as fencing, to deny access to the shadow's area.

INFILTRATION

Badges are one of the most common methods for reducing industrial espionage's penetration threat. Unfortunately, it is a far from foolproof method. Relying on the front guard station to review large numbers of employee badges each day, to issue visitors badges, to answer the telephone, and to carry out other duties stretches the badge system to its limits. As we shall see in Chapter 7, stealing and creating badges is not all that difficult to do. In addition to posing as an employee with a badge, other common infiltration techniques include:

- Posing as a refuse collector.
- Impersonating utility employees.
- Joining an office cleaning crew.
- Working for a vendor that services the copying machines, etc.

While the badge system and the front desk guard's desk both act as deterrents, additional internal lines of defense become necessary. In Chapter 8 we will discuss developing internal "porcupines" that will collide with and stick into a spy that leaps over the perimeter defenses.

SALES FORCE

A competitor's intelligence gathering force isn't limited to professional spies. Talking to a wide range of people, including a target's employees, sales people are natural intelligence gatherers. What they obtain may be gossip on occasion, but valuable intelligence comes their way too. John D. Rockefeller's Standard Oil Company in the 1880s used its sales force to track competitors' sales. Standard Oil also located low-level employees for competitors such as bookkeepers. They bribed those employees to provide inside data on sales and production figures. Since the sales force travels around, rubbing elbows with representatives from other companies can help identify inside sources in other businesses.

A sales force trained in gathering intelligence can obtain the following information:

- Learn about expansions in the physical plant or in the size of the target's workforce.
- Acquire information about upcoming marketing plans and sales promotions.
- Identify employees recently "let go" or who left the company because they were dissatisfied. (These persons may possess valuable information and "loose tongues.")
- Identify current employees who could be recruited as information sources.
- Learn about problems with products or product lines. (The target cannot meet current demand. Demand has fallen off. Or, parts or materials shortages exist making production difficult.)

Sales forces picking up on this inside information has been going on since companies started employing sales professionals in the nineteenth century. They exchange stories with suppliers, other vendors, managers, purchasing agents, other sales people, administrative staff, and technical employees. Often, they acquire considerable intelligence data without raising much suspicion.

Certainly, training employees to be on guard against this intelligence method may help some. But, everyone has to realize that the twenty-first century economy depends upon a flow of information to function. We can't cut off our businesses from the rest of the world. Some information "leakage" will occur, despite our best intentions. The best counterpoint may be to gather intelligence effectively ourselves. We'll deal with this issue in Chapter 9.

TRASH RAIDING

Digging through the trash is a fundamental investigative and intelligence technique. Hackers do it. The police do it at crime scenes. Private investigators make it a standard operating practice on many different types of investigations. To a spy, it offers observation inside a target like an archaeologist putting together the puzzle of an ancient civilization.

The simplest methods to defeat trash raiding are to pulverize, to shred, and to destroy sensitive papers and computer media before they hit the trash bin. If clients cannot do this themselves, then hire a professional shredding service. But, remember that the problem doesn't stop with shredding and then with locking up the corporate trash bin. Documents have to be stored securely prior to destruction. And, as indicated earlier in the chapter, employees in the field have to employ secure document and computer media disposal procedures. Never assume trash raiding will not go on. It is too easy to do for a spy to skip the practice if your client makes the information accessible there.

PUBLIC RECORDS

In Chapter 2, we discussed sources of technical and business information about companies. Chapter 5, "Multi-line Attacks" will discuss the sources of information available about individuals. Personal information becomes intertwined with business data. For example, license plate numbers can lead to the names and addresses of key employees. With the growing number of databases commercially available, less and less of a person's "information sphere" remains private. Since people tend to base passwords and other identifiers on information from their private life, teaching employees to keep their private information sphere separate from their corporate one is important. Vital records (birth, deaths, and marriage), motor vehicle records, criminal histories, real estate transactions, corporate affiliations, recreation vehicles owned, and credit history are all up for grabs by industrial spies.

The personal information can leverage the cracking of passwords or be the basis for recruiting employees in personal difficulties. Employees need to realize that these information handles exist. They should report anyone probing into their background and any recruitment activity by outsiders.

CLOAKING

Cloaking is security's neglected handmaiden. It hinders, blinds, and misleads observation. Blunting the sense of sight, cloaking makes the industrial spy's job harder, and at times, it cuts off the intelligence gathering process. To cloak requires added steps in storing goods and in manufacturing; perhaps, this is why it remains neglected. But, with a bit of ingenuity, cloaking can become part of an industrial routine.

What can be cloaked? We've discussed laptop theft. Carrying a laptop in travel luggage other than your normal laptop carrying case would cloak the machine and deter theft. If the thief doesn't see the carrying case associated with laptops, then he or she will assume you do not have one. A knapsack, a gym bag, or conventional travel luggage act to cloak the laptop. So, placing small things inside relatively larger containers cloaks them. Making the small larger or bulkier is a fundamental trick of the cloaking trade.

How does one cloak information? If a user places a sensitive file on a directory amidst many other similar files (not in content, but in name and type), that action blends the sensitive file into routine, unexceptional surroundings. Encryption of the file still will be necessary as an additional safeguard, but the spy will have a much harder time finding it. Locating file marffgg1765.1231001.tz in a haystack of marffgg1765.0000000.tz to marffgg1765.2100000.tz, when there are no clues that marffgg1765.1231001.tz is special, is very difficult to say the least.

Misinformation is another cloaking ploy. Much like Stoll's phony technical file, placing flashy decoys on your information systems will divert the spy's attention away from the real data placed in an obscure directory with a boring name. Information in paper form should be stored in a secure but low-key fashion. Don't place them in a room with the sign on the door, "Sensitive Document Storage." Avoid signposts when ever feasible.

If a container has labeling or distinctive markings that give away its sensitive contents, obscure those markings or place the contents in a different container. If neither of those options is feasible, store the container inside in an area not accessible by the public or visitors.

When shipments arrive of materials, parts, or components that could give clues as to processes that are trade secrets, make the items arrive by common carrier and not in the vendor's truck. Arrange to have packaging for such items to be as nondescript as possible. If such items must stored outside, try to mix or to intersperse them with similar non-sensitive items. When that step is not feasible, cover the items with tarps to cloak what they are or contain.

If smoke emissions, releases of water, or increases in power use signals that sensitive processes are running, try to schedule these production runs at night to reduce their visibility. Ramp up power use gradually, if possible, to avoid sudden telltale spikes in consumption. Avoid the testing of proprietary products or processes outdoors if at all possible. If absolutely necessary, improvise cloaking materials to obscure the equipment used or tested.

Travel by key technical staff or by executives reveals a great deal about what a company is doing and planning. Make sure the company uses a bonded travel agency that has signed a confidentiality agreement. Arrange a procedure for the secure delivery of travel documents to the company. When executives meet for sensitive negotiations or discussions out of town, try to arrange the meetings in a neutral location like a hotel that has high traffic. This meeting place will at least partially cloak who is involved.

The fundamental action verbs for cloaking are, (a) hide, (b) distort, (c) misdirect, (d) decoy, (e) camouflage, and (f) blend. Hiding something does not always mean placing it in a super secure, secret place. Often people ignore the commonplace. Don't hesitate to be creative here. Distorting an object, like with the automotive test vehicles, makes observation unreliable. Stoll employed decoys and misdirection, an electronic sleight of hand, with his phony technical files. Placing a red box containing sensitive materials with other nonsensitive red boxes camouflages or blends the object into the environment.

DISCUSSION

1. Develop a plan for cloaking against aerial surveillance of a site you are familiar with. Be sure to include specifics of what actions you would take.

2. How could you cloak emissions like smoke from industrial processes other than running them at night?
3. Charles, an employee in the computer design lab, goes on lunch break and forgets to log off his terminal. Sheila, a technician in the lab, who does not have authorization to access the lab testing database, piggybacks on Charles' terminal. She copies several key files onto a diskette. Later on her lunch break, she hides the diskette behind a food vending machine. Her boyfriend, Carl, who works for the food vending machine company, acts as her "cutout" when he services the machine the next day and retrieves the diskette. Describe the countermeasures you would employ to defeat this scheme.
4. Do some research on the Internet, and in the print media, on an executive that you know at a local company. Write a brief summary of the personal information that you accumulate. (See Chapter 7 for more background on this issue.)

FOR FURTHER READING

1. *Running a Ring of Spies* by Jefferson Mack, Paladin Press, 1996.

2. *Secrets of a Super Hacker* by the Knightmare, Loompanics Unlimited, 1994.

Chapter 5

MULTI-LINE TECHNIQUES

In 1855, Allan Pinkerton's detective agency was actively engaged in investigating industrial espionage cases for the railroads in the Midwest. The railroads were the first complex interstate business in America. With industrialism's new complexity came the commercial spy. Large-scale industrial operations require specialization. With specialization, the multitude of operations necessary to run a railroad demanded various occupations: engineer, brakeman, switchman, conductor, and so on. An enterprise like the railroad required gathering information from different workers and departments to gain a total intelligence picture. Complexity required developing multiple avenues for industrial espionage. Observation served spies well, but other sources of information were emerging. Comparing those sources of the nineteenth century with those of today, we find some interesting similarities:

1. The introduction of telegraph communications, which could be "tapped" and monitored. (Today, the targets are telecommunications, cellular telephones, wireless computing, and the Internet.)
2. Newspapers provided mass information for the first time. (They are still with us, supplemented by electronic media and databases. In fact, databases create a collective power for print media far beyond what any one newspaper or magazine offers. The fictional Sherlock Holmes kept newspaper accounts in his "commonplace books." They served as a chronicle of 1880s London to research during his investigations. He understood the cumulative power of indexing articles over time, which foreshadows the immense power of a LexisNexis or a Dialog.)

3. Exhibitions introduced technological developments to the general public in the late nineteenth century. Alexander Graham Bell, for example, demonstrated his telephone at the 1876 Centennial Exposition in Philadelphia. (Today, trade fairs and technical meetings occur on a regular basis, providing valuable intelligence.)

4. Administrative documents increased at an unparalleled pace in the late nineteenth century. The amount of paper generated by business and government required the expansion of professions such as law, accounting, management, and the clerical forces. As industrialism grew in America, information became a commodity to be created, processed, organized, stored, and most important, retrieved at will. Information was no longer the domain of the elite or the privileged, but it became a currency handled by the common worker. (Today, so much information exists, new professions have emerged: the information broker, the business intelligence analyst, and the information professional [formerly known as librarians]. Today's industrial spy may be a blend of all three professions.)

SOURCES OF INFORMATION

Claude W. Olney in his article, "The Secret World of the Industrial Spy" *(Business and Society Review,* Winter 1988, Issue 64), identified 20 classical sources for the industrial spy. Let's review some of his ideas and add a few of our own to the discussion. This will serve as a recap of some previous material and introduce some new concepts.

1. Information (Knowledge): (a) Published Material (open sources). This domain includes printed and electronic media from journalistic sources. It also includes public records (whether in print or electronic form) such as motor vehicle records, real estate transactions, and vital records of births, deaths, and marriages. (b) Published Financial Reports. These reports are corporate annual and quarterly reports. And, the documents include those filings available through the Securities and Exchange Commission's EDGAR database at http://www.sec.gov/edgar.shtml. (c) Industry Analysts' Reports. (d) Corporate Brochures and Pub-

lications. (e) Independent or Privately Commissioned Marketing Surveys and Consultants' Reports. (f) Purloined Technical Drawings, Reports, Lab Notes, and other Proprietary Documents. (g) Technical and Scientific Literature Published in Journals and Magazines. (h) Tangible Things. Physical objects can carry information. For example, in a recent case at University of California, Davis, a former university researcher faced charges for allegedly stealing vials of biological "glue" used in stem cell experiments.

2. Observation: (a) Sales people submitting intelligence reports from the field. (b) Trespassing on the target's premises. Infiltration and trash raiding. (c) Electronic eavesdropping. (d) Attending open meetings, conferences, and social events. (e) Computers as spy tools. (f) Aerial surveillance and satellite imagery. (g) Factory tours.

3. People Techniques: (a) Employment interviews (legitimate and false). (b) False licensing negotiations. (c) False acquisition or merger negotiations. (d) Hiring an employee away from a target to learn what is in the employee's head. (e) Planting an agent in a company. (f) False flag recruitment. (g) Social engineering. (h) Camouflaged questioning at technical meetings. (i) Hiring professional spies or private investigators to find out background information on key employees. (j) Bribery. (k) Using sex, blackmail, or threats to gain information.

The ideal operating environment for the industrial spy rests upon deep knowledge of the target's key employees. Deep knowledge also encompasses the financial, technical, and operating specifics for the business. Integrating these two "deep knowledge" pools together produces an "information horizon" around the target. Founded upon the horizon's knowledge base, the spy has multiple lines of attack against the target. Think of all the items of information publicly available about the business and its people as spokes of a wheel. The rim of the wheel represents the information horizon of the business where all the seemingly unrelated pieces of information about the business reside. These primary facts lead a spy down one or more of the spokes to the hub where the sensitive information resides.

A multi-line attack starts with general background research on the target. Perusing news accounts, help wanted ads, and company publications, a spy gains a general overview of the company's organization and operations. Then, the spy moves from the outer rim toward the hub and accesses less public information. Getting his hands on a corporate telephone directory, a spy now has a guide to the organization. It helps to locate telephone numbers for the mailroom, the computer operations center, and departmental numbers with the names of rank and file employees. (A telephone directory need not be in print format. It can be in a section on the company's Intranet site. If a spy is fortunate, the electronic telephone directory will also include email addresses, department affiliations, and even instant messaging addresses.) This information provides stepping stones to secrets.

With a directory of employees at hand, supplemented by background investigations of key employees, a corporate spy may conduct social engineering to move down the spokes of the wheel. Social engineering convinces people via telephone or email that a spy has a legitimate right to know something. A piece of information like a password, the name of a file, the location of certain documents serves as a stepping stone. Combining flattery, an air of confidence, sheer bluster, and the smooth talk of a charlatan, the spy nibbles away at information security through social engineering until little remains.

By telephone, a spy impersonates legitimate employees, plays the part of a manager or a supervisor, and acts as if she were a customer or vendor with a need-to-know. With good background research, pulling data from the horizon or rim, she possesses enough information to sound convincing. She obtains logins and passwords by claiming she's forgotten them and she's in a "jam." "Can you please help me?" will be the refrain. Combining the right amount of an appeal to pity and the pressure of urgency, the caller often gets what they ask for. Employees may say, "Oh, I'm really not supposed to do this, but I'll give you a hand since it is an emergency." Or they'll reply, "We'll do it just this one time, but in the future see your manager." People want to be helpful, and they hate to say "no" to imploring voices.

Similar tactics obtain access to confidential records, faxed information, corporate credit card purchase records or numbers, and even Federal Express® or UPS account numbers. A call to the mailroom could go, "This is Carl Jackson in the tech lab. I'm filling out 2 Federal Express pouch here, what is our account number?" By sounding authoritative yet routine, the spy can access all the keys to the kingdom via social engineering. And, with accurate facts such as a Carl Jackson in the tech lab really exists, the spy sounds for real. Attacks can be on different people in different departments, each supplying a fragment for the puzzle's solution, and none the wiser for it. A spying campaign can combine knowledge attacks, observation methods, and people techniques across the spectrum of the company and thus be truly multi-line.

Imagine that a spy calls a clerical person in your business research unit. By telling a convincing story that he is auditing database usage, he obtains the online service's account numbers. With this information, the spy can contact that service. In the contact he is able to obtain a three-month printout of database inquiries. From this information the spy can determine the focus of the company's competitive business research. What companies are they looking at? Which databases receive focus by the target? These are important clues to the thinking and the concerns behind the business intelligence effort. Similar techniques work for almost any kind of utility records or vendor invoices.

Larger, complex organizations are more prone to multi-line techniques. Often one department or section remains totally ignorant of the events in another section. A "divide and conquer" approach works best where a target generates competing fiefdoms and departmental turf rivalries. Calling different people in the organization to gather "information fragments" becomes much easier under those conditions. Employees do not tend to get together and compare notes when inter-departmental conflicts are the norm. Seemingly unrelated fragments build a picture to a trained eye. Where many will see ambiguity in bits and pieces derived from different sources, an intelligence specialist generates patterns from the same data.

An industrial spy's stock-in-trade is to perceive an information path through your company or organization. Flexible, accepting of setbacks, understanding zigzags and sidetracks, the industrial spy has a mindset quite different from traditional corporate America. Security with a bureaucratic focus assumes an information thief will try to attack in the manner scripted by the security force. Spies write their own scripts.

The poet, Robert Frost, spoke of taking a different path in "The Road Not Taken." Henry David Thoreau in *Walden* mentions marching to a different drummer. Ralph Waldo Emerson implores in "Self-Reliance" on the importance of being a nonconformist. Expect all of this from an industrial spy. For a spy will take the road or path you didn't plan for or anticipate. While a security professional shouldn't try to be a clair-voyant, emulating a potential attacker's thinking remains within the reach of brainstorming. Bruce Schneier in *Secrets & Lies* argues that the creative security professional can discover unusual paths to information by using what he calls "attack trees." Building an attack tree starts with the trunk: identifying the most common methods of theft. Add branches for the less recognized methods. If necessary, graft on branches to those branches to represent a path that may be rather unusual. Via brainstorming sessions, envision a penetration route through the tree to sensitive information.

A spy's attack commences with a single news account. Susan Crisp, the CIO (Chief Information Officer) for Diversified Biometrics, during an interview for a biotechnology journal, reveals Tech Advocates as their new public relations firm. By reading the interview, the spy sees Tech Advocates as a backdoor into Diversified Biometrics. Doing some background research on Susan Crisp, the spy learns that she is married to a Richard Crisp, and the couple has one child, Peter, age 12. This information arises from doing an "alpha" search under Susan's name in a commercial motor vehicle database. The search produces a 2002 Volvo registered to Susan Crisp and to Richard Crisp.

A check of news articles on the LexisNexis database uncovers several about Susan. One of the articles is a profile that identifies Susan's husband. Consulting the marriage database from again a commercial source, the spy learns that they were married in 1987. A back issue of the company's newsletter found in the public library's corporate collection on local businesses identifies in a "bio" piece her son Peter, age 11 at the time. Running "Peter Crisp" on a birth database for their state of residence yields 2/19/90 as his date of birth.

Using this information, the spy finds the Web site for Tech Advocates via an Internet search engine. On the Web site the spy discovers a "Customer/Client Login" section. He goes for the obvious for the login. After all the Web page says, "Enter in your seven character login." And, the system accepts "DIVBIOM." Using variations on Susan's name and on her family information, the spy tries "SUSRICH," "SUSPETE," "SUSAN1987RICHARD," and "PETER1990" as possible passwords. He has no luck yet. But, with a little more experimenting, he tries "RICH87," which gets him into the client area for Susan's company. Once in the client area, the spy finds documents related to the target's marketing plans, and even R&D progress reports.

One objection to this fictional account may be that Susan Crisp, as a CIO, would not use personal information in passwords. While a CIO should know better, my experience with IT professionals is that they are often no better or worse than the rest of us, at least as far as always having their guard up. They face the same problems as many ordinary users: too many pieces of information to remember. It becomes natural to use the same password in different situations. Convenience will always be in conflict with security.

Little pieces of information grow into branches on the attack tree. (See Figure 5-1.) The prize may be on a very high branch. But an information thief can follow a path up the trunk and through the forks in the branches to the prize. Or, perhaps the spy can jump over from a neighboring branch like in Susan Crisp's case. Several security measures may have blocked this attack:

1. A password-checking program that detects easy-to-guess passwords would prevent short, vulnerable passwords like "RICH87." Simple to implement on Diversified Biometrics' system, however, the attack occurred on a vendor's Web site. How much control can a customer exert on a vendor's security practices? Contractual requirements are a possible avenue to insure a level of protection.

2. Another step is not to place proprietary documents on Tech Advocates' database. While this measure provides ultimate protection, it may be cumbersome for business. Encryption could afford a high level of protection. But, of course, the vendor's people need the ability to decipher the documents. Will they be able to keep the cryptographic keys safe?

3. Why does Susan Crisp need access to this information? A strict need-to-know policy would bar her unless she regularly needed access to do her work. Giving blanket access to certain classes of employees only widens the universe of possible attacks. But, political and power concerns within a company may make such restrictions difficult.

Protection of information in a highly connected world of electrons cannot ever be free of paradox. Constructing attack trees can help us envision multiple lines of attack. But, our response usually cannot be total and absolute. For every countermeasure taken, technical, business, and political concerns weigh against complete effectiveness. We must allocate resources to the most probable threats, but leave a degree of flexibility in responding to the unusual. Brainstorming by the secu-

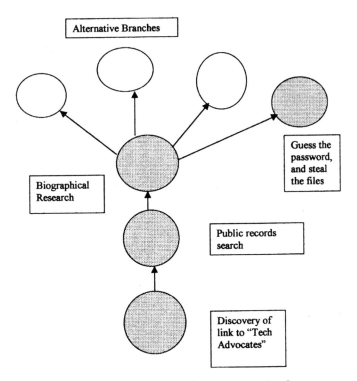

Figure 5-1. Attack Tree (Susan Crisp Case)

rity professional becomes a powerful tool to remain supple in our response.

BRAINSTORMING

Suggesting that a security professional acquire brainstorming skills ventures not so much into new territory but one without many guide-posts. "Be creative" is easy to say. We work in a grinding environment of many daily demands. A general admonition to brainstorm solutions doesn't go very far. So, let's look at some specific ideas.

An initial approach involves thinking like a thief. Rather than just admire security defenses, think of ways around them. Things that are familiar though don't always cry out with their defects. Seeing the comfortable, the well known, as something strange requires some practice. Taking a different perspective is key.

Rather than just rummaging through the mind's closet looking for "creative approaches," consider exercises to make the process more focused. Grasp an everyday object like a pen. List ten ways you could use the pen as something other than as a writing instrument. The access card in your wallet will get you into your own building. Think of three ways it could get you into another company's building. Consider multiple alternatives. Focusing in on a single solution too early blinds a team to alternative paths in resolving the problem. For example, in a recent episode of the ABC television show, *The Mole,* the contestants faced the problem of trying to move a small French automobile inside a shed. The shed's sliding door was open partially, wide enough for two people to walk through, but a padlock secured the door. Prohibited from damaging the door or the lock, the team elected to disassemble the automobile part by part and carry each part through the narrow opening. They focused on the auto. Midway through the disassembly, a team member examined the lock and noticed it was a combination padlock. They checked the odometer on the auto. Then they dialed the odometer reading into the lock, and it opened. By looking at the problem from a different perspective, they were able to push the auto inside.

In assessing security problems, start with a central concept. But, don't be afraid to look at the concept from different angles. For example, in the Susan Crisp scenario, ask the fundamental question: "Where is our information vulnerable outside of our walls?" Generating this central concept question is not always an easy proposition. It can invite criticism by members of your security staff or from people in other departments. Positive self-criticism creates uneasiness for sure, but the practice may be the only way to discover the unconsidered.

Assume you've had a brainstorming session about your defenses. While generally things seem to be going fairly well, your staff expresses some concerns that sensitive information, albeit with authorization, travels outside the security perimeter. At this point, the issue now requires some expansion and digging for details. The first step would be identifying the extramural handlers of sensitive files. A preliminary list includes:

1. *Vendors.* Consider the people who actually work with the data like Tech Advocates and the transporters of the information such courier services.

2. *Suppliers.* These companies may need access to sensitive specifications in order to deliver the necessary components or raw materials.

3. *Consultants.* The persons may have to take sensitive information with them to do research.

4. *Government and Regulatory Agencies.* They may handle sensitive information to process permits, licenses, product applications, and so on.

5. *Telecommuting Employees.* Not only do they take home sensitive documents and files, but also the remote accessing of sensitive electronic data is becoming the norm for this group. Many companies use a VPN (Virtual Private Network) to allow the safe transmission of data over the Internet, but are these workers keeping their end of the connection secure? Most people feel secure in their homes, so leaving computers logged in but unattended is a real danger. Also, password security remains a real question. Are passwords scribbled on the desk pad? Is the corporate password the same one the employee uses for accessing personal ISP providers such as Prodigy, AOL, and the like?

6. *Traveling Employees.* These persons face similar dangers to those of the telecommuters. They also face a greater risk of computer laptop theft. And, while hotel rooms may afford psychological security, in reality many people have access to your room in a hotel. So, these workers need to be careful regarding what they leave in their rooms, especially in the trash.

Once the brainstorming session identifies likely targets, focusing in on specific attack paths is the next step. Word play with action verbs, relational words, and noun objects is a useful tool. Here are some verbs that reflect general actions:

Multiply	By-pass
Divide	Generate
Add	Invert
Cut	Separate
Submerge	Throw
Jump	Copy
Soften	Expand
Freeze	Probe
Harden	

Almost any strong action verb can play a role in brainstorming. Some of the ones from the security vocabulary include: penetrate, steal, spy, infiltrate, hide, observe, eavesdrop, distract, purloin, encrypt, retrieve, guess, and divert. Combined with relational words and noun objects they form "threat phrases." Relational words denote direction, location, or connection between an object and a verb. Common relational words are: about, above, amid, around, below, beside, opposite, through, toward, via, while, with, and without. Common nouns or objects pertaining to security are: data, alarm, laptop, firewall, alert, lock, guard, fence, computer, network, password, perimeter, camera, access point, penetration, diversion, telephone, access card, and so on. "Infiltrate computer center via purloined access card," "distract security guards through parking lot diversion," and "guess password by probing employee's personal data" are examples of possible threat or attack phrases. (See Figure 5-2.)

For example, we can force relationships between the various elements in the Susan Crisp case:

1. Probe personal data.
2. Amid news reports and records much personal data.
3. Personal data submerges into password.
4. Vendor's passwords not hardened.
5. Infiltrate through Vendor's Web site.
6. Sensitive records not encrypted.
7. Records copied by spy.
8. No alerts generated by penetration.

These conjunctions of ideas can be the product of random juxtaposing of verbs, nouns, and relational words. Constructing a table for each category as in Figure 5-2 will be useful. The goal is not to craft a final form of security measures from the word play exercise. Rather, it is a tool to stimulate thinking from different perspectives, to make the familiar seem strange, so some new analysis will be possible. Don't be judgmental too early. Discard ideas only after they have received adequate consideration and a bit of kicking around. Try to develop a pattern from disparate elements. Think of how someone could climb that tree.

Brainstorming takes time and effort, but it can uncover vulnerabilities not considered previously. Just remember brainstorming involves creating lists and then examining the interrelationships between those lists. How do those relationships force new thinking about the central

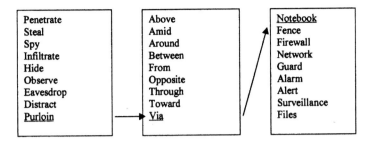

Figure 5-2. Brainstorming Words. (Stealing computer files.)

concept? Use these word association exercises regularly to stay creative in recognizing your vulnerabilities. A good practice is to incorporate new keywords into the association exercises when your intelligence gathering produces news accounts or reports of new attacks or threats. Threats will continue to evolve. Keep your security vocabulary in step with the information thieves.

FOREIGN SPIES

Foreign spies use the techniques and play the same games as domestic industrial spies. They certainly exploit any advantages that open records can afford them with facts about the target. Recruiting nationals from their own country to act as spies remains a common practice. University and college students here on visas are prime targets. After they finish their degrees, they find their way into research programs in academia or in major American corporations. And, there isn't much that security can do about preventing this scheme, other than to be aware that it does happen. Compartmentalizing sensitive information as much as possible is the best countermeasure. Keep information dissemination as much as possible on a strictly need-to-know basis. Make sure access to the research lab is not carte blanche access to all your company's research information. (See Chapter 6, "University Research Ploy.")

Another concern about foreign intelligence agencies gathering economic intelligence is their aggressive tactics overseas against American business people. Executives traveling to Europe and Asia especially should never feel comfortable in their hotel or meeting rooms. The rooms may be bugged, the trash examined, and their telephone tapped. The rule of thumb should be never leave anything with valuable information content unattended in a room or in a restaurant overseas. If bringing sensitive information along on an overseas trip is necessary, make sure a security professional accompanies the executive to guard sensitive information when the executive is absent from the room.

The executive should refrain from sensitive discussions over the hotel room's telephone or within the room itself. Also, don't use cellular telephones for similar communications. Always assume that the infrastructure will be in place to do electronic eavesdropping at will in a foreign country.

Foreign spies will also reach around the world via the Internet. If they can obtain information via newsgroups, chat rooms, and bulletin boards, they may be able to pose in cyberspace as employees of American companies. They may be asking for help online about a technical problem they've been working on. Instructing your employees to be leery of information requests online from people they do not know enhances your information security program.

TARGETS AND TRENDS

What are the targets and trends in industrial espionage for the twenty-first century? What key industries will spies be targeting? The prime targets are:

Aerospace
Biotechnology
Software
Automobile Manufacturing
Pharmaceutical Manufacturing

Software piracy will continue as a growth industry for the foreseeable future. Countries in Europe and in Asia will remain as key players in this global infringement of intellectual property rights.

The Russians in the 1980s gathered intelligence on radar for the United States Air Force's F-14, F-15, and F-18 aircraft and for NASA's space shuttle. Aerospace technology will continue to be a hotbed of industrial espionage activity in the twenty-first century.

The next wave of the post-industrial revolution will be in biotechnology. The need to develop new drugs, crops, and vaccines will insure that area of knowledge remains a highly competitive environment. A recent news account in the *Austin American-Statesman* about the alleged theft of materials involved in stem cell research indicates that this is a very hot area for spying.

The pharmaceutical and automobile manufacturing sectors have been targets for some time. We should expect no abatements of activity in these areas for the foreseeable future.

While the listed industries are prime targets, the security professional needs to keep in mind that any business can be the target of industrial espionage. All that is required is a competitor who is jealous of the target's intellectual property.

DISCUSSION

1. Ira Winkler comments in *Corporate Espionage* that the main threats to information assets will not be from technical vulnerabilities but "through operations, physical, or personnel exposures." Describe how sources of information discussed in this chapter play a role in three avenues of attack Winkler identifies.
2. In what ways can a company's or a person's information horizon be reduced? Describe in detail any methods you suggest.
3. Create an attack tree for penetrating a computer system or network that you are familiar with.
4. Develop a multi-line attack against an information asset in your company or organization.
5. In industrial espionage, are any countries friendly? Or should every foreign power be viewed as an adversary? Explain your answer.
6. Conduct a brainstorming session with fellow workers or students on laptop computer theft. Cover both the possible consequences of these thefts and countermeasures to mitigate any losses they cause.
7. Write a scenario of how a spy could use publicly available information to launch a social engineering attack on your organization.

Chapter 6

POWER AND POLITICS

Nothing occurs in the American corporation without power or politics as a major factor. Conducting security operations without recognizing this guiding principle invites peril. The security professional need not engage in power plays. He or she must often remain neutral. But, political savvy, understanding what can happen, often differentiates the superior protection specialist from the mediocre.

Much security training concentrates on physical security techniques. These concepts form the profession's knowledge base, which we will review in the next two chapters. Abandoning that knowledge base is not this book's message. Rather, given the protean and fluid quality of the Digital Age, the text suggests supplementing physical security methods with intelligence gathering tools and political insight. Intelligence methods create new eyes and ears for incipient threats emerging on the horizon. (We'll cover those methods in Chapters 8 and 9.) Political cognizance helps the security professional appreciate the pulling, baiting, prodding, and twisting of human emotions that emerge from power struggles.

Political training teaches the reader about protecting his or her back. For a variety of reasons, as strange as it might seem, managers in your own company may try to sabotage the security effort. Some managers may mouth the cliché, "There's no 'I' in the word 'team.'" Yet, they are very much into the pronoun "I" and all else is secondary. To understand this paradox requires examining the lines of power security will encounter within a company. The first line or axis of power revolves around the desire for convenience. Security procedures prevent the ease-of-use for information systems, physical assets, and other resources. Some employees and managers constantly seek ways to bypass security measures they deem "inconvenient." They scream and complain if security encroaches upon their fiefdom.

This first power axis causes hassles and discomfort for security professionals. Found in most businesses, these backbiters will be the bane of any corporate security department. Obviously, diplomacy, tact, and a thick skin enable one to deal with these individuals who need to grow up a bit. Some tolerance of pettiness goes with the job. And at times, even the backbiters have some legitimate concerns. Stay on top of things and make sure legitimate complaints get resolved. Be courteous, but don't be afraid to speak the truth with these individuals when you know you are right. Rarely will this power axis pose a serious threat to a security manager's job if the manager is doing the job correctly.

The second axis has heavier implications. Manipulating human weaknesses, spies use bribery, deception, and sex to pry information from lower-level and middle management employees. Looking for the dysfunctional personality, recruiters in the intelligence game identify employees with two characteristics. First, the employee has access to sensitive information. And second, they have a personal problem that the spy can resolve, at least on a temporary basis. That problem may entail gambling debts, other financial troubles, sexual or marital problems, or substance abuse.

Employees often mask these problems to their employers, but when they get out into the world after work, the mask disappears. Corporate spies employing some creativity identify potential recruits. They find the recruits at the places where they play. Using open sources (public records and news sources), they build a dossier on potential targets. They pull strings with contacts in the financial industry to see the target's credit records and billing statements. From those records, they identify when the subject shops, gambles, drinks, pursues sexual partners, and otherwise recreates their money away. With this personal information, they learn where to eyeball the potential recruit in action. The approach from this point varies, depending upon the circumstances. Usually, the spy tries to befriend the targeted employee and to create a dependency.

This second, hidden power axis is particularly insidious, because everything happens below the surface. The compromise first of the employee and then of that employee's loyalty take place outside of the company's walls. When the employee starts stealing information within your walls, security gets their first opportunity to discover the scheme. Very often though, theft goes on for some time before detection happens. These compromised employees operate under security's radar, unless an internal security net is in place to catch them. Unless internal intelligence programs described in Chapter 8 are working, these insiders chew like termites through your information assets.

Compromised employees may exploit security vulnerabilities created by the first power axis. A defiant manager may create a lax security environment, where rule bending becomes the norm, and this attitude generates vectors for stealing information. Such omissions add up to an information buffet for the insider spy.

The third axis of power works from above rather than below. Security's vantagepoint assumes that most threats emerge from the lower levels of the organizational pyramid. Certainly, entry-level and middle-level employees, traditionally at least, possess the financial motivation to commit internal crimes. Nonexempt employees, other nonmanagerial workers, and first-line supervisors are all under security's watchful eye.

Yet, industrial espionage corrupts the top levels too. Spies and their clients build alliances at the lower levels with "small money." At the executive level, they gather allies with "big money." Spending far less than what R&D would cost them in the long run, a predatory company wins influence with executives through "investments," "new business," "the promise of new business," and offers of lucrative personal advancement. And, if the carrot does not work, threats to harm existing business can do the trick. An executive losing a major account faces the loss of prestige, a drop in income, or possibly his or her job.

A company desiring to steal proprietary data or trade secrets may actually send some business the target's way. Often, an executive within the target gets credit for securing a new account. That executive becomes an "advocate" for this new business "partner." After building this relationship with the executive, the predator has some "insurance." Should security question the new customer's motives or actions, the executive may run interference for the "account" or try to impede an investigation.

If a company uncovers industrial espionage activity by a competitor, it may determine that civil legal action is the best remedy. Even then, the predatory company may see a financial advantage into buying their way out of trouble. They may approach members of the board with offers of purchase or investment. An effective tactic against smaller or medium-sized companies not publicly held, paying off from above kills an investigation. Security needs to be aware that most business people are in business to generate wealth, not to stand on principle for principle's sake. This is not meant as a cynical observation but as a statement of reality. We have to deal with men and women as they are, not as our wishful thinking would like them to be.

Executives are not immune from personal difficulties. They get into the same "jams" as other employees. So, they can fall prey to bribery or compromise too. This situation, while sad, is probably the most contained. If an executive betrays the company purely out of self-interest, then building a coalition to protect his or her position will be problematical at best. Only when an executive *appears* to be acting in the best interest of the company will the actions be worthy of defense. (Appearance versus reality, that is the great paradox of what can happen in the executive ranks.) In that case, probably none of the executive's colleagues will dare call it betrayal.

An attack along the third power axis threatens security's rear and flank simultaneously. The security professional, undermined from behind and left without allies, shudders in the quiet. Being backstabbed from the top is, to borrow a phrase from Tom Clancy, "the sum of all fears." From day one on the job the security professional must build alliances and working relationships with a broad spectrum of the company's management. They provide options in the event of an internal power play. Without such resources, however, the security professional could face deafening silence when assembling forces against a strong internal foe. Also, avoid a multi-front war. Don't neglect problems on axis one and axis two. Collect intelligence, take effective action when needed, not letting those areas get out of control. If you do face a third axis attack, concentrating on it won't be the problem. You'll not have to stamp out multiple fires.

BRIBERY

The industrial spy has used bribery since the beginning of the Industrial Revolution. John D. Rockefeller Sr.'s Standard Oil Company in the 1880s bribed competitor's bookkeepers about oil sales. Standard's spies gathered details from grocers, distributors, and railway-freight agents on every barrel sold by independents. Payoffs and bribery were the tools of an industry giant to stay on top of its competitors.

In 1997, Bristol-Myers Squibb in Philadelphia became the target of two Taiwanese men who allegedly tried to buy inside knowledge about manufacturing methods for Taxol. This anti-cancer drug was an intellectual property sought after by Far Eastern pharmaceutical firms. The case fell under the *Economic Espionage Act of 1996,* which made stealing trade secrets a serious crime. It also made industrial espionage by foreign governments a grave crime, carrying a sentence of 15 years in prison.

As mentioned before, the bribery technique need not happen only at administrative level. Executive and lower-level employees can succumb to a bribe's temptations. Regardless of the target, bribery schemes leave common signs or indicators. Suddenly, the employee's financial tribulations abate or disappear. Spending increases on luxury items or pursuits. The employee works longer hours and starts having after-hours visits to the office. He or she may start asking questions about areas or projects outside of their normal responsibilities. If resistance develops during normal inquiries concerning possible security compromises, then the investigator should have strong suspicions.

Isolating a bribery scheme requires a two-pronged approach. First, identify the employee that co-workers consider the "information leak." Document in interviews the specifics of why they suspect the individual. These facts should include:

1. Changes in working hours and working habits.
2. Unusual activities such as excessive checking out of sensitive documents, excessive photocopying, or excessive time spent on sensitive databases or in computer files.
3. Taking home unusual numbers of documents.
4. Spending long periods in his or her office with the door closed. Acting withdrawn from co-workers or being "startled" if someone comes into the office or cubicle "unannounced."
5. Unusual requests for information from other departments. Or, asking co-workers to find out information outside of the norm or beyond the regular requirements for the department's mission.

The inquiry's other prong should document changes in lifestyle. Sources of information will be supervisors, managers, co-workers, business associates, neighbors, and creditors. Obviously, any inquiries conducted need discreet handling. Always tell information providers that the matter is a routine inquiry, a background check. The clearest indicator of something is amiss comes with an abrupt reversal in financial fortune. Repossession efforts suddenly cease. Creditors stop telephoning. Collection efforts disappear. At the executive level, the suspect has new business ventures or investments. Though often, these business interests may remain undisclosed to the executive's employer.

A complete background investigation to reveal links to undisclosed business interests and to other assets will be necessary. (See "Background Investigations" in Chapter 10.) Developing documentary evidence to prove that changes in lifestyle and financial condition originate from an unknown source acts as the keystone in a bribery investigation.

Once the two prongs of a bribery investigation converge on a single person (or a group of individuals), the documented facts need review by the highest level of management. The corruption of the suspect must be the only logical explanation for the theft or compromise of proprietary information. It is critical for the security professional to remain totally objective in the presentation. Sticking to the facts, the security professional must avoid any bias toward a particular faction, department, or section within the company. If upper management concurs with your findings, they may authorize limited surveillance on the suspect to identify the bribing parties.

Such surveillance may cover monitoring electronic communications like company email, company telephones, Internet access from the company's computers, and the use of workplace instant messaging services via the Internet. Eyeball and video surveillance on and off the company premises is a possibility. This surveillance must not be illegal or intrusive. It must conform to the company's rules and disclosures to employees about when they may be observed. In addition, all surveillance must not violate state or federal law and regulations. Electronic surveillance, outside of the company's premises or facilities, will require law enforcement's involvement. They will conduct any electronic surveillance subsequent to court orders or search warrants.

Any bribery investigation requires a strong trust relationship between a security manager and high-level management. This relationship becomes even more critical when an investigation may involve an executive within the company. Such trust emerges from the security professional's daily commitment to honesty, high integrity, keeping confidences, and fair dealing.

DISINFORMATION

Usually, we view industrial espionage as a matter of stealing information assets. But, destroying, blunting, or denigrating an asset's value confers, in some cases, similar advantages to a competitor. When stealing proprietary data remains chancy, an unscrupulous competitor may choose, instead, a disinformation campaign. The Internet Age allows rumors to travel at light speed around the globe. Often, little time exists to weigh carefully allegations or rumors promulgated through cyberspace. With careful forethought, the planting of allegations that a company's products contain defects or pose safety hazards could cause tidal waves of suspicion by the public. Suspicion impedes or halts investment, cancels orders, pushes regulatory approval to the rear burner, and implodes retail sales.

Disinformation targets aren't just products or research projects. Key individuals in the company, including the security manager and the security staff, are all possible targets of a disinformation campaign. Again, with the Internet's available resources, appearance versus reality comes into play. Appearing to send or receive child pornography, hate mail, and libelous communications destroys a reputation. Appearing to engage in insulting or accusatory emails with customers, suppliers, vendors, or co-workers demolishes business relationships. Imagine the impact of distributing managerial salaries throughout the company's email network. Consider what happens if the emails bear the sending address as that of the security manager. The Vice President of Operations appears to send a bulk email to major customers accusing them of cheating when paying their invoices. Or, the director of a major research project having his photo and a testimonial posted on a Web site supporting racial supremacy of whites over blacks and Asians.

Subtle, endless variations exist on the disinformation tactic. Any twenty-first century enterprise needs to recognize its potential destructiveness. Industries particularly vulnerable to this discrediting tactic are:

1. Those companies engaged in genetic research. (Wild stories of mutant viruses and bacteria incite public hysteria.)
2. Nuclear industries. (Allegations of faulty safety measures or of contamination.)
3. Pharmaceutical firms. (Safety problems with drugs or allegations of contamination.)
4. Food producers and distributors. (Allegations of contamination.)
5. Computer manufacturers. (Faulty hardware or microchips.)
6. Software manufacturers. (Bug-ridden software, software failures.)

Of course, we are talking about false allegations suddenly appearing on the Internet. Inquiries by legitimate organizations like governmental agencies, responsible consumer groups, and responsible journalists are a totally different matter. Disinformation campaigns require a response developed and planned well in advance of any crisis. This ultimate power play by an adversary demands a reasoned, professional counterattack, which is difficult to do under pressure. The chances for coping with an emergency like this improve with good preparation. Those preparations should cover the following areas:

1. Have forensic services in place to determine the actual origin point of emails and Web postings.
2. Establish a crisis management team to contact customers, vendors, regulatory agencies, suppliers, and the media with the correct facts.
3. Create the ability to deploy rapidly a rumor hotline to handle inquiries by customers, the press, stockholders, business partners, and employees.
4. Establish an investigative team to separate fact from fiction regarding the allegations.
5. Insure that the media or public relations unit has the capability to issue timely announcements on the Internet and to the press during a crisis.

TRADE SECRET THEFT

Chapter 10 will discuss at length the legal aspects of investigating a trade secrets theft case. At this juncture we ask, what a trade secret is and how does it differ from confidential information? A trade secret holds proprietary information essential to the business; the public does not know the specifics of which. And, patent, copyright, or trademark protection does not exist for trade secrets. Secrecy is their protection. Access to trade secrets remains on a strict need-to-know basis. If a company neglects this secrecy, then the courts may hold it was not in fact a trade secret. Mere confidential information does not qualify. A company would not reveal to the public the social security numbers of its employees. But, that information is not a trade secret. The compromise of social security numbers could create legal liabilities for the company, but that compromise, in and of itself, does not cause grave harm to the business' bottom line. Yet, someone learning the recipe for a well-known brand of cookies or for a famous soft drink could cause serious financial harm.

The security manager should work on document control procedures regarding the handling of trade secrets. The best system tracks the location of trade secret data at all times: who had control over the information and when they had control. Sensitive information, which is not a trade secret, requires careful handling but not the highest and most stringent controls. Compromising a trade secret deprives the company of an exclusive right. Whereas the divulging of sensitive information creates legal or public relations problems, but these consequences usually fall short of catastrophic to the bottom line. To prove to the courts that the item stolen was a trade secret, it must cry out as critical to the business, and reasonable documentation must establish the controls placed on the information.

Good document controls will include:

A. Dual control of trade secrets. One person alone should not be able to handle and remove the documents.
B. Tight sign-in and sign-out procedures. Both authorized persons must be present to complete these steps.
C. A secure work area for highly sensitive documents and trade secrets. It should be physically and electronically isolated from the rest of the facility.
D. Twenty-four hour security or monitoring of the storage area for these secrets. (Usually via an alarm system and video surveillance.)

E. Finally, electronic transfers of trade secrets need protection with strong encryption and by transfer through a secure channel like a VPN (Virtual Private Network).

Whenever dealing with other businesses where discussions involving trade secret information become necessary, always obtain nondisclosure and confidentiality agreements. These executed agreements make it clear that all the parties involved understood that the information was an asset needing protection. Because a common power move is to pretend interest in a buy-out, merger, or an investment, protect the client by being on guard. Document access to the information by an outside party.

UNIVERSITY RESEARCH PLOY

If your company contracts part of its research efforts to a university, then make sure that the contract covers security issues. (The procedure applies to third-party research facilities and independent testing labs too.) In addition to nondisclosure and confidentiality agreements, certain data protection standards should be in place. Please note that students and research fellows from around the world are visiting major American universities. Foreign corporations and domestic competitors also fund university research programs. Make sure that your data remains as compartmentalized as possible.

Foreign governments in Europe and Asia encourage their science and technology students to attend American universities. (And, in all fairness, American students do go to those countries to study as well.) These foreign students in America sometimes act as eyes and ears for overseas powers.

Under the guise of academic freedom and inquiry, American universities can become treasure chests of innovation and technology for foreign spies. Be careful to insure that research programs conducted outside of your portals follow these guidelines:

1. Physical and electronic separation of different projects. This safeguard includes both records and research personnel.
2. Proper storage facilities for proprietary data and documents. Locking up data is essential.

3. Adequate access controls to computer databases. The use of pass-words and encryption as needed.
4. Access controls to research labs and work areas. One project's badges and access cards should not allow entry to another project's areas.
5. Security audits done jointly by the university or the independent lab during the life of the contract.
6. The right of final approval on any persons granted access to restricted areas or information.
7. Exercise the right to have unannounced security inspections.

PATENTS

In Chapter 2, we discussed patent analysis as a tool for determining technological leadership. In addition to being an analytical tool, patents enter the power game in infringement and in squatting cases. A smaller company may hold a patent on technology needed by a larger competitor. Outright infringement, coupled with other espionage activities, seeks to gain total leverage over a smaller competitor. The infringed party may face a long legal battle to assert its rights and to prove the infringement. Meanwhile, the competitor earns substantial profits, royalty-free, off of the other company's ideas.

The classic case remains Marconi's pirating of Nikola Tesla's radio plans from the U.S. Patent Office in the early 1900s. Tesla sued Marconi in 1915 for the patent infringement. The United States Supreme Court in 1943, 28 years later, upheld Tesla's patent numbered 645,516 and determined that it anticipated Marconi's four-circuit tuned combination, which served as the basis for modern radio. Patent fights take time, resources, and research to win. A bullying point in the intellectual property game, unscrupulous companies will infringe patents.

The security manager needs to make sure that management understands the mere existence of patent doesn't insure protection against corporate spying. Even with patent information available, there will be gaps in knowledge necessary to pull off the infringement. Industrial espionage goes hand-in-hand with patent infringement. Therefore, a strong information security program can be a good deterrent to infringement. All of the ancillary technical, procedural, and production information that allow the patent's ideas to go into manufacture need to be treated like a trade secret. Keep that information secure, and infringing upon the patent will be difficult.

A word needs to be said about "patent squatting." In this scheme, an individual or company obtains a legitimate patent. But, instead of manufacturing a product or licensing the patent's technology, they proceed to litigate against every deep pocket that comes down the road later, using a technology that even remotely resembles the one in their patent. The goal is to obtain settlements or to sell licenses to the companies that they sue. While this practice is not illegal, and it is certainly not industrial espionage, it is another tactic to be aware of in the intellectual property game.

RUSES AND DECEPTION

Deceptions beckon like the serpent with the apple. If the approach has enough sugar or if the person making the pitch sizzles, many of us can fall for the scheme. Getting our guard to drop, getting us to bury our skepticism, the spy vaults over the toughest hurdle. What's in the industrial spy's deception toolkit? The primary tools exploit beliefs, persuade with cover, and dazzle with sex.

Deceptions based upon belief allow the "dupe" to think they are doing something worthwhile by "helping" the spy. For example, the "false flag" recruitment plays upon the employee's sympathy for a cause. A worker may believe that his company engages in practices that harm the environment. The spy may approach the employee as an environmental activist. Meeting at an environmental rally, they have a subsequent series of coffee shop "bull sessions." During these sessions, the spy convinces the employee that he knows a key aide on the United States House Environmental Subcommittee. If the employee brings him inside data on the company's genetically engineered crop research, he'll see the aide gets it for the committee's review. Eager "to make a difference," the employee agrees to help. Actually, the data the employee purloins ends up going to a competitor and not the United States House subcommittee. A smart spy will play the story out with the employee, so the "dupe" isn't any the wiser. He will claim the information was turned over to the subcommittee, but they have "decided not to act on it at this time." Even if the deceived employee later discovers the truth, he remains powerless to act without revealing his own involvement.

Cover stories persuade others that the spy is someone else. (A short-term version of this ploy is social engineering, discussed in Chapter 5 Long-term cover often involves contact with the target over weeks or months.) An industrial spy may pose as a headhunter, a graduate student doing research, a co-worker from a different region, or as a journalist. Building a plausible cover requires documentation and preparation. With today's desktop publishing programs, the cornucopia of corporate, academic, and governmental logos available on the Internet, and portable laminating equipment, forging credentials and documents is not difficult. Preparation involves research, so the spy can talk the part. And, quite a bit of that research material resides on the Internet on almost any subject. In the Internet Age, contact with the "mark" can begin by email, via newsgroups, and through Web sites. Personal contact often originates at conferences and seminars. Sometimes, a series of friendly telephone calls will do. By talking the part, people usually accept even a newcomer at face value. After a while, they let their guard down. Before long, they'll exchange email after the initial meeting and end up doing favors for the spy. And, it can be all nonthreatening and friendly with no bribes and no promises. Based upon being likeable, having some charm, and a plausible story, people will open doors, retrieve information, and get that "misplaced" or "forgotten" password for the spy.

Sexual deception often overcomes people of either gender with varying sexual tastes. Regardless of the target's education, religious background, or business ethics, the logical faculties fall prey to the emotional and hormonal dimensions. With the right stimulus, people act rather than think through the situation. Sex and espionage combine the two oldest professions.

During the Vietnam Era, nightclubs in Saigon and in other parts of the country catered to the social needs of American servicemen. This tawdry side of warfare occurred in other conflicts to be sure. It thrived in South Vietnam. Some of the establishments in Vietnam were actually intelligence collection points for the Viet Cong (VC). When one considers how inexpensive they were to operate, the GI's paid for the alcohol and the sexual services; it was a great deal for the VC. Conveniently located near American military bases, the women employed at the VC bars, engaged in "pillow talk" after entertaining their customers. From this chit-chat, the VC learned about troop movements and their strength, operations, and force deployments.

The same tactics work at the local watering hole near your client's company. Sexual operatives, hired by spies, develop relationships with targeted employees. Sometimes these relationships are just barroom conversations; people will reveal a lot when an attractive person shows an interest. If necessary, the operative may start dating the target with the view to acquire information over the long-term. When sufficiently "hooked," the target will face recruitment by the operative. The emotional wedge forcing the employee into betraying the employer is the threat of losing the dating partner. A ruthless, inhumane practice, unfortunately it does happen and can be quite effective.

Sexual deception is a difficult area to develop countermeasures against. The panacea for industrial espionage remains the catchword "education." But, from a practical standpoint, conducting training sessions on sexual espionage can appear "overblown" and become embarrassing for all involved. A less sensational approach encourages employees to maintain healthy skepticism when meeting new people, whether in business or in one's social life. People who seek them out deserve some scrutiny. Don't teach cynicism; just encourage them to be cautious. Investigate the claims of any stranger should be the standing rule. If anyone tries to recruit them for industrial espionage, they should report it to security immediately. It may be the employee's only chance to avoid a trap he or she cannot escape alone.

WHAT THE VIETNAM WAR TAUGHT US

Our intelligence efforts during the Vietnam War were considerable, but they failed to anticipate the Tet Offensive in 1968. The Viet Cong emerged out of "nowhere" to strike at South Vietnam's major urban centers. Although the offensive ultimately failed militarily, it caused a decline in American confidence at home. That decline resulted in the eventual withdrawal of American forces. The Viet Cong won the propaganda war, the battle for public opinion.

In analyzing the Tet Offensive, Colonel John Hughes-Wilson, in *Military Intelligence Blunders* (Carroll & Graf, 1999), identifies four areas that contributed to the American intelligence debacle. Those areas include:

1. *Turf squabbles.* Different branches of the services and various intelligence services could not see developments leading to Tet with a common vision.
2. *Managerial mindset.* Americans are good managers, but they often fail in trying to understand an opponent's mind. The bureaucratic solution fits all circumstances regardless of other factors.
3. *Bureaucracy.* Dotting all the bureaucratic I's and adhering to all the paper shuffling details interferes with keeping tabs on a fast moving enemy.
4. *Warfare is not just a numbers game.* Tracking enemy killed or guns seized may yield some interesting statistics, but it doesn't mean the enemy is losing and that you are winning.

American intelligence gathering in the political and military sphere continues to suffer from myopia. The collapse of the former Soviet Union and the terrorist attacks of September 11, 2001 both came in under the radar. We can also throw in the fall of the Shah of Iran and Iraq's invasion of Kuwait. Getting the big picture remains a problem for the American government's intelligence community.

What then are the similarities between government intelligence gathering and corporate endeavors? Corporate America remains bureaucratic, political, and possessed by the managerial mindset. The average American corporation seeks to quantify, whether in numbers or in dollars, all of their projects and operations. Certainly, to varying degrees American corporations host turf wars between internal departments and groups on a regular basis.

Since industrial espionage does not appear on the radar every day, its damage is not always apparent or quantifiable. The industrial spy often remains invisible, the greatest source of his or her power. For the spy exploits infighting between departments to an advantage, but the security manager must operate in spite of them. A security manager has a difficult sales job convincing an executive to devote money and resources to combating a quiet, often hidden threat. And, that executive may be embroiled in his or her own struggles to preserve power among warring cliques and factions. Industrial espionage threats often seem distant.

The mastery of politics may not appear a part of the security professional's job. Remaining politically neutral in turf wars should be a standing maxim. A security professional's mission is to protect all of the company, not just a few likeable sections or departments. Yet, becoming an astute politician in persuading managers is a vital skill. The security professional should always strive to speak the truth. Managers who shun negative information on a regular basis invite danger and remain difficult to serve. Clinging to the self-delusion that things are different than they really are only creates a perilous work environment for the security professional. Without the ability to give effective counsel, the security manager at best possesses a blunt sword. The security professional ventures on a constant odyssey to find leaders in the company who will listen to his or her counsel and who will trust a professional's opinion and reputation.

In times of crisis, like an attack along the third power axis, the ability to have those in power listen to and trust what the security professional says can mean job survival. Cultivate those relationships at every chance. Develop a reputation as not being a bureaucrat, but as someone who can get things done with an even hand. Shun the worshippers of bureaucracy when events demand immediate, decisive action. Speak clearly on what needs to be done. Equivocation, bureaucratic-couched talk, and mealy-mouthed expressions will make you appear weak. Something you can't afford.

DISCUSSION

1. You have an investigation underway regarding a competitor that is launching a similar product. Your company was thought to have a substantial technological lead in this area. An inquiry begins. As the investigation progresses, the director for West Coast Sales starts raising objections to the inquiry. What is your plan of action?

2. An employee in the genetics lab approaches security with the concern that the lab's manager has started acting "strangely." He has become less communicative with fellow employees. In the recent past, his habit was to work a fixed daytime schedule; now he comes in at odd hours at night too. He acts defensively when

asked about what documents he has in his office. The informant thinks the changes in behavior began a month after the manager started dating a new girlfriend. Outline your plan for investigative action. (You may want to consult "Background Investigations" in Chapter 10.)

3. Research a hostile takeover from press accounts, business journal accounts, and other coverage in the media. List the power tactics used in the takeover bid.

4. Outline a security audit program for an independent research facility under contract with your company.

5. A journalist doing a book on the biotechnology industry wants to interview some of your technical staff. Describe the steps you will take to verify the journalist's identity and to protect your proprietary information.

Chapter 7

COUNTERMEASURES

Seeing things with new eyes is the goal for this chapter. We suspend, for the time being, any belief that countermeasures solve security problems. Dabbling in this heresy, we hope to envision how the information thief bypasses defenses. Taking this approach runs certain risks. First, some among the orthodox may feel that showing a thief vaulting over security measures will only encourage their breach by others. In the Information Age, there are few security secrets that stay secret for long. Today's rogues remain well ahead of us in developing techniques to overcome countermeasures. Our general discussion will not provide aid and comfort with which they are not already acquainted.

The second concern is whether the security professional's ethics become compromised in adopting a criminal's point of view. Profilers working on behalf of law enforcement use this approach without any corrupting influence. A security professional can do the same without fear of becoming a criminal.

Finally, some worry that concentrating on the weaknesses of countermeasures will undermine confidence in the profession. Recognizing limitations never undermines security. As a profession we have never promised absolute security for anyone. The wisdom of the profession dictates that we afford different levels of protection based upon available resources. Invincible defenses we are not. Any security measure may fall short under the right circumstances. The challenge becomes adapting quickly to shortfalls with backup plans or with changes in strategy. The battlefield doesn't offer set piece engagements where the enemy attacks according to our wishes. Rather, we strive to protect clients in a fluid theatre of evolving threats and changing perils. Looking at the dark side of countermeasures may not be pleasant, but it can be enlightening. So, let's listen to our fictional spy.

THE INFORMATION PREDATOR

My attack on the company occurred at several levels. The target wasn't "easy pickings." They had security, which required some thinking of their part in advance, but it wasn't enough. It is not that I am the smartest person or that they had feeble intellects. Rather, I was persistent. It was a job for them, a challenge and a game for me. I got to push my creativity to the edge and more.

Learning to think and look around the corner enables me to sidestep obstacles when the target wants me to walk straight ahead. Respect for the opposition allows me to survive as an industrial spy. But, I realize that quite often I'm up against bureaucrats, who may be competent in their jobs, yet, deviating from the game plan poses difficulties for them. Usually, they are hamstrung with procedural minutiae. I have a game plan too, but very often it is far more pliable. Many times I rewrite the target's game plan to suit my needs.

Sometimes winning this game just requires being at the receiving end of what the target throws your way. Companies are giving away their critical, sensitive information, and they don't even realize what's happening. Computers are being thrown away, sold or auctioned off, or donated to charity with valuable data still on the hard drives. With nearly 500 million computers becoming obsolete by 2007, used computers present a sizeable waste management problem for businesses. Many users think that simply "deleting" the files solves the problem. It doesn't, but they still feel comfortable in trashing them or giving them away once "obsolete."

My target tossed the older machines into the dumpster. The mildly obsolescent they donated to local schools or to Goodwill. However, security considerations did come into play before disposal. Using an off-the-shelf sanitizing program, they "wiped" the hard drives. These wiping programs claim to write over every iota of disk space. Unfortunately for the target, these run-of-the-mill erasure programs are not one hundred percent efficient. They can miss significant amounts of data.

Several machines from the target's software development lab left on the loading dock contained a huge number of megabytes. Due to an oversight, they were not actually erased. Yet, having been marked "junk," the cleaning crew placed them on the loading dock. The workers leaving them outside didn't have the keys to the locked trash bin.

Computers given to charity received only cursory security handling. Reformatting the drives, which sounds thorough but really isn't, was the extent of the cleansing process. The local thrift store sold the machines to the general public. And the target's machines were easy to spot. Someone had forgotten to remove the distinctive inventory tags on the back of the machines. For some small sums, I purchased several computers. At home, I used a free unformat program and retrieved a treasure chest of proprietary data.

Some users think that replacing sensitive data with large amounts of innocuous material destroys everything on the drive. For example, overwriting a hard drive with an old encyclopedia off a CD-ROM appears to do the trick. Actually, considerable slack space exists on hard drive. Since records do not perfectly overlap each other during a rewrite, significant amounts of data still exists between files. And of course, magnetic remanence, the magnetic induction remaining after the magnetic field has altered the disk, still allows reconstruction of data. Forensic computer specialists with law enforcement recreate extensive records from slack space all the time. Advanced computer forensic labs also restore faded magnetic images from disks even when they have been "degaussed."

In many cases all one needs to read the complete contents of a disk is a HEX editor. It gives a read-out in hexadecimal and in ASCII English text. (ASCII text is raw text without any word processing formatting.) You can read everything on the hard drive, especially records or files the target thought were long gone. The same method works for floppy disks and other removable storage media.

Shredded documents normally keep away prying eyes. In this area, the target's research staff did a commendable job of being consistent in shredding documents. However, they made a few mistakes. First, they didn't mix nonsensitive shredded documents with the sensitive shredded material. Second, the shredder made one-quarter inch (1/4″) linear cuts only. No angle cutting or pulverizing occurred. And finally, they didn't use a secure disposal service. We were able to retrieve the plastic bags from an unlocked trash bin. It took some reconstruction, but we were able to paste together significant documents. Once shredded, the documents didn't receive an additional level of randomness. And, the thinking probably went that once a document is shredded, why bother to secure it until burned?

If you have enough persistence, keeping an eye on loading docks and storage areas, locating documents in waiting for shredding occurs fairly often. A research unit has several boxes of documents that need destruction. They move the boxes on first shift into the hallway and mark them "Please Shred." Security officers on the third shift normally collect these boxes and see that the contents get "chopped." However, on second shift, the janitors need to treat and buff the hallway's floor. The boxes are in the way. Figuring that they are just trash, the janitors put the boxes on the dock. Missteps in the document security process happen all the time. A good spy just needs tenacity and patience to spot these information "goofs."

Copy machines and their attendant work areas beckon me like a Tom Clancy thriller or a Robert Ludlum spy novel. Employees invariably leave sensitive materials and documents around the copying venue. Keeping a sharp lookout when you pass one of these areas may yield a lab report, financial information, marketing data, and so on. It only takes seconds to purloin or to copy one of these prizes. The security force does check these areas during the day and even more so during the evening hours. Unfortunately, the security force does get sidelined handling broken sprinkler heads in the warehouse, exterior doors ajar, employees locked out of their cars, and workers needing first aid.

In fact, I can keep the uniformed security force quite preoccupied in the evening hours. Some of my favorite entertainment for them on the "late night spy show" included:

1. Calling two or three pizza delivery services and ordering food for nonexistent, or even better, daytime employees. When the pizzas arrive at the front desk, the nighttime security officer can spend a lot of time sorting out if these people are working late and where they are in the building.

2. Put a small amount of liquid coffee in one of those glass coffeepots. Turn the electric service burner on, and place the pot on it. After a while, the coffee burns into an awful carboniferous residue. The wonderful burnt odor wafts throughout the build-

ing. Security officers then have to spend time checking all the coffee stations looking for the offending pot. Then, they have to do some cleanup to dissipate the odor. The trick buys you some time to do some snooping in another area of the building.

3. Jam an exterior door open, which sets off an alarm at the guard station. This trick is particularly effective when there are only one or two security officers on duty. Jam some duct tape or paper in the door's catch plate. It will take some time for the security officer to free the material out of the catch plate's opening. He or she may have to retrieve a screwdriver from somewhere to do the job. Do this at a door where employees step out for a smoke. Security will think employees rigged the door to allow for an easy "in and out."

4. Have an associate disturb vehicles in the parking lot so that car alarms go off. Invariably, part of the security force will go outside to investigate something that they cannot do anything about. For a variation on the trick, loosen the valve stem on a parked car with an alarm. The air will leak out slowly, which will periodically trigger the alarm as the car's level drops due to the deflating tire.

5. Disable video surveillance cameras. Sometimes this is as simple as throwing a switch on the camera or unplugging it from the wall. This action will tie up security trying to figure out what is going on. Meanwhile, you can pry into files at the other end of the building.

6. Trigger a sprinkler head or set off an alarm in area away from where you will be snooping.

Diversions are limited only by the spy's imagination. Put a strain upon limited security resources. Take advantage of the unexpected. I witnessed a third shift manufacturing crew and its security force thrown in chaos because a bat got into the building and flew around inches above worker's heads. (This event provided an opportunity to slip away and to penetrate restricted areas.)

Security people pride themselves in using locks and physical barriers to keep out spies and unauthorized individuals. Any time you see a padlock, think opportunity. Most padlocks, unless they are military, NASA, or nuclear facility quality, cut right off with an industrial-grade bolt cutter. Those with boron-hardened steel shackles will require a

power-assisted bolt cutter. Even a high security padlock can resist a dia-
mond-edged saw only for a period of time. If a padlock secures something valuable, cut it off, then substitute your own lock, which you can
unlock at will later. This tactic is useful in low traffic areas. On patrol,
security will see a lock in place and not be any wiser. If during a penetration security spots you, their barriers can protect your retreat. Locking the rear gate behind you with your lock with leave them with a gate
they can't open, barring their pursuit.

Picking inset door locks requires some locksmith knowledge, but
learning that skill is far from insurmountable. However, purloining
keys or making copies of keys offers a better strategy. Often, you can
explain why you have a key, but explaining a lock pick kit may not be
so easy. And, picking a lock takes time, leaving you exposed. Many
companies have poor key control. Someone leaves keys on their desk
or on the dash of the car. Or, the key control box is left unlocked at the
receptionist's desk. Keys are available if you keep an eye out for them.

Office furniture locks in the age of the cubicle are notoriously inse-
cure. Armed with a heavy-duty screwdriver, a spy will find many draw-
ers and overhead cabinets pry open easily. If an information thief
desires avoiding any signs of a break-in, obtaining office furniture keys
is not difficult. The keys are available in office furniture stores and on
the Internet. Someone just needs to know the make and the lock number. The lock number is stamped into the metal on the face of the lock.
If it is hard to read due to limited lighting or the location of the lock,
take a piece of white paper, press it against the stamping, and rub the
paper with a lead pencil to pick up the stamping. Most of the inset locks
on metal cabinets work the same way with a stamping on the lock's
face. Just don't get too cute about building a collection of keys. Running around with a key chain of furniture keys dangling from your back
pocket will attract security's attention. And, unless your cover involves
servicing office furniture, you can't explain why you have them. So, be
conservative in their use.

Fences and physical barriers offer a degree of psychological comfort
to the target. Frequently though, they're just for show. Few companies
want a perimeter of eight-foot high, heavy-gauged wire fencing topped
with razor-sharp barbed concertina and patrolled by guards with trun-
cheons and side arms. Aesthetic considerations generally come first, so
most barriers remain scalable even by the minimally athletic. As indicated in the prior discussion, most padlocks, at best, are a nuisance to

a spy. True, barriers and perimeter defenses increase in strength with alarms and sensors. But these systems are often expensive to deploy and to maintain. They also cause their share of false alarms, which can serve as diversions too, if properly timed. In addition, thunderstorms reduce the effectiveness of perimeter video cameras and alarm systems. Storm activity limits visibility and increases false alarms. Bad weather can provide a good cover for an exterior penetration.

A technical assault on a gate, lock, fence, or other barrier may be far inferior to capitalizing on weaknesses in human perception. When trying to penetrate a construction site, dress like a construction worker with jeans, a work shirt, work boots, a hard-hat, and a work belt. To enter an access-controlled facility, find the congregation point for smokers outside the building. Dress to blend in with the crowd. Wear a facsimile of the company badge that you created from your desktop publishing program. Leisurely walk up to the group just like you are coming back from your car. Have a smoke, and then go inside with the group. Sometimes, you can skip the acting by finding exterior doors left unlocked or propped open to accommodate smokers. (As long as there are smokers, back doors will exist into targets.)

Once past exterior barriers, internal access control points requiring a badge scan will succumb via piggybacking. Wait for several people wanting to enter the restricted area. Invariably, the first person in line runs his or her badge, and everyone else piles in behind. Just join the crowd.

Another option in the access badge game is to steal access badges from handbags and coats left on counters and under tables in bars and nightclubs. Ladies generally don't take their purses to the dance floor, and gentlemen usually shed coats and jackets before dancing. After a few drinks, people stop being so careful about their plastic. Being observant of the parking lots' pavement around such establishments, near the target, often yields badges fallen from pockets and purses. In the summertime, windows to cars may be left rolled down with clip-on badges lying on the dash or dangling by a lanyard from the rear view mirror. Reconnoiter the nearby drive-up ATM machine or the self-service gas pumps. I've found fallen badges, driver's licenses, and credit cards at both places. People are more careless and fumbling than you might think.

As amazing as it sounds, most badges and access cards provide excellent clues as to where to use them. I've found badges and access cards in parking lots that provided the name of the employee, the name and location of the work site, and the identity of the internal access point ("Computer Lab Access"). Who said getting into controlled access areas was difficult? True, these "lost cards" will get reported, usually on Monday, after the weekend hangover subsides. By that time, the penetration already has been done and the goods are out the door.

By-passing physical security requires a bit of imagination but not *Mission Impossible* skills or gadgets. Figuring out computer passwords hardly requires a computer science degree from MIT or Cal Tech. Most of the time, they are written down somewhere not too far from the computer. Start with looking under the keyboard. (Of course, as the text indicated in Chapter 5, social engineering provides another good nontechnical way to get passwords. So, we won't have our spy cover this territory again.)

A more technical approach to defeat passwords requires using a brute force program. This program tries a large number of passwords from a special dictionary of the most commonly used passwords. Since most people choose short, easy to remember passwords, these brute force programs usually get the job done. They can take some time to set up and try, not hours of course, but use your judgment in employing one when you are under a tight time constraint. Passwords that are highly resistant to brute force attacks possess both length and randomness. If the user employs a random password generator, he or she may have a password that can withstand brute force methods. So, knowing as much as possible about your targeted user beforehand determines whether a brute force attack would be advantageous. But, remember few people use a password like "1940745ttrEccugtY36zjETUY." Far more people use one like "DALLASCOWBOYS." The first one is long and random. And, the second password may be longer than the usual length of about six characters, but has a low level of randomness due to deriving from popular culture.

ROAD MAPS

When gaining access to a company, whether through employment cover, posing as a third-party vendor, or by outright illegal entry, the "maps" a target provides will astound you. Most companies have extensive "signage" on doors, in hallways, in meeting rooms, on filing cabinets, and on walkways between buildings answering two fundamental questions. Where is everything? And, what is this? Most companies do little masking or cloaking of their operations. Provided you observe carefully, if certain equipment is in use, you quickly learn that certain manufacturing operations, or perhaps research experiments, are under way. Other signs include the sudden consumption of raw materials or the arrival of supplies on the loading dock. A job on the receiving dock should be a   sought-after position for a spy. All manner and means of the target's affairs become manifest there. Packing slips, shipping bills, and the labeling on boxes tell stories to rival John Le Carre's novels.

Companies may employ a background check on workers. While these checks may screen out common-law criminals, guilty of robbery, larceny, burglary, or violence, they will have little effect on me. I am neither a highwayman nor a mugger. If I did have a criminal record, I would hire people with clean records to spy for me. Background checks won't keep me out.

If you gain access inside a target under cover, check out the security functions within the business. Are the security officers effective? How often do they patrol the premises? When they are on patrol, do they appear observant? Are they checking key locations throughout the business such as the copy centers, computer labs, record storage areas, and so on? Or, do they spend their time socializing with the opposite sex, taking excessive breaks, or even napping? Answering these questions prior to conducting "intell" operations can make all the difference in having a smooth, undetected gambit.

In keeping tabs on security officers, note the times of their absence from key security points: the front desk, video security monitors, posts at entrances to critical labs or production areas, and presence in the computer facility. When they are away, are they actually on patrol or are they just goofing off? Are their patrols highly predictable? Or, do they vary their paths and times through the building?

Trace one of their patrols. In their wake do you find sensitive documents still near the fax and copy machines? Are the doors to executives' office remaining unlocked? Are filing cabinets unlocked? Do you find contraband such as drugs or alcoholic beverages stashed away behind vending machines, hidden at first aid stations, or placed above the ceiling tiles in the locker room? A "yes" answer to any of these questions indicates the patrols are ineffectual. Running an intelligence operation on the premises probably won't encounter much opposition.

A WORD ABOUT COMPUTER SECURITY

Some companies believe that the heart of any information security plan rests in IT or network defenses. If network access controls are strong, then an information thief cannot get far. Network security focuses on keeping hackers out. The IT program's effectiveness against industrial spies remains problematical. Tight network security controls do pose formidable barriers to intruder wannabes.

However, concentrating solely upon electronic safeguards ignores the fact that most data will reach paper form. Paper documents require extensive, cumbersome safeguards in order to protect them. They need physical security from creation to destruction. To information predators like myself, getting around physical security isn't all that difficult. I can attack paper documents at any time in their life cycle. My primary directive is to always look for paper documents in storage. Or, I look for ways to get them printed, so they are no longer within the IT perimeter of protection.

I consider any business as having three perimeters for information security. The first is the exterior physical security barrier. Many companies stop here. If you penetrate the exterior defenses, you'll find a fairly easy time inside. The internal defenses such as the security force, internal locks, internal access controls, and surveillance systems are the second barrier. If the effort at this level is superficial, then again a professional industrial spy will have few problems. The final layer of security covers measures taken within the IT system to protect the network and individual computers. Since computer security remains a hot topic in corporate America, expect some professional effort here at good defenses. The defense watchword, however, is "good" not "insurmountable."

Assuming total computer security at any facility invites folly. Computer security will always fall short for the following reasons:

1. A large percentage of passwords and logins are not that hard to guess or to crack. To maintain a high level of password security

requires a Herculean effort with constant friction against human nature.

2. Workers leave their systems logged in while they go on break or to lunch or even when they leave for the night. Piggybacking becomes a tactic fairly easy to employ.

3. People with high-level access can be compromised by bribery or by threat of reprisal.

4. Once data stops being electrons and takes physical form on paper, microfiche, unencrypted files on disks, or stored on tape, it becomes much easier to steal.

Some IT countermeasures do cause me problems. I keep an eye out for the following:

A. Good password controls. (Passwords are long, unpredictable in content, which means a high level of randomness, and get changed regularly.)

B. Audit controls are in place. All network activity gets logged. (To check and see the extent of this activity, piggyback on someone else's login and try to access a file they don't have privileges for. Check later to see if they get a security email about it. A one-time attempt shouldn't cause much of a stir; it will be dismissed most likely as an error.)

C. The network has good segmenting using firewalls, proxy servers, and routers. (If you go into your MS.DOS window, you can't change the drive directory to drives and servers outside of your segment.)

D. Effective encryption is in place. (Files and databases are encrypted using publicly tested encryption algorithms like Triple-DES, and PGP. Look for policies regarding encryption on the company's Intranet site. Emails transmitting public-keys, the use of PGP in emails, and employee training classes on encryption procedures are all signs of heavy encryption use.)

E. Network intrusion detection is in place. (Do a buffer overflow attack on the target's network login software. Try to go on the system a few days later using the same attack. If you can't do a login, it is a good sign intrusion detection is going on and logs are being checked regularly.)

If your initial survey indicates weakness in any of these areas, you may be able to develop a strong vector for attack. But, if the target employs vigilance in these realms, bringing a computer security specialist to assist in the penetration may be necessary. Unless, of course, the compromise of an insider is possible, and it eliminates the need for outside help.

DISCUSSION

1. The security specialist functions in a corporate environment, but he has to think beyond corporate culture. Explain this paradox in the light of developing countermeasures.
2. Is it true that most security systems operate in the failure mode? (The criminals always seem to stay ahead of us.) If so, can countermeasures be devised which stay in front of the industrial spy?
3. Why is the security specialist's shadow the best protection for a client's facility? In what ways can the security force's interdiction of industrial espionage activity become unpredictable to the industrial spy?
4. How could intelligence gathering activity by security limit the "safe space" for industrial espionage operations?

FOR FURTHER READING

1. For further information on the erasure of computer media, check out Data Security Research's site at http://www.redemtech.com.

2. For a security survey from a traditional security perspective, consult James F. Broder's *Risk Analysis and the Security Survey,* 1984, available through the Certified Protection Professional program at the American Society for Industrial Security.

Chapter 8

INTERNAL INTELLIGENCE

This chapter counterbalances against the last, where we showed countermeasures as opportunities for the spy. Here, we start talking about crafting roadblocks, creating perils for the spy. Industrial spies enjoy great flexibility in the manner of their attacks. But, security professionals can reduce spies' comfort zones through proactive intelligence measures. The spy's narrative now focuses on how security disrupts the espionage campaign by its own form of snooping.

THE INFORMATION PREDATOR CONTINUES

Companies that are difficult to penetrate have one overriding characteristic. And, it isn't that they possess the latest biometric access device or video surveillance system. Rather, they don't rely on perimeter defenses alone to keep me out. They have an attitude. To borrow a term from basketball, they employ a "full court press."

In the first place, they use spies too, on the inside. And, those spies are looking for the likes of me constantly. These internal spies may be trained security officers in uniform gathering intelligence. Or, they are informants, people who have regular jobs in the company, but have special training to look for the signs of industrial espionage.

Whether they are in uniform or not, they exist to make my life difficult. I don't know who has their eyes out for me, and that undercurrent of worry narrows my comfort zone. I can't move around with the freedom I enjoy in most companies. Constricting of my activities creates problems. For example, I want to get inside a secure room that contains the target's software development servers. If I manage to disable the area's air conditioning, at most places staffers unlock the door, and they direct portable fans on the servers until the air conditioning resumes. After the fans' placement, the development staffers go tend to other business. Meanwhile, I slip inside the room and run a backup tape to copy some critical data off one of the servers. Not exactly *Mission Impossible* or James Bond, but the scheme works. Unless, the company knows what it is doing. In that case, they post someone to watch the server room until the AC comes back on and they lock the door.

I know I have potential risks, when after causing a diversion, the security force does not lose focus. Staying on their toes requires the security force to think like I do and be flexible. They understand threats change as the day or night progresses. What may be important to do at 8 a.m. may have to be put on hold at 3 a.m. when the security staffing is limited. They also understand that they are there to protect certain assets, and distractions from that mission are not going to get the best of them. That kind of determination causes problems for me.

If I were teaching security personnel on how to combat industrial espionage, I would tell them to learn how to defeat boredom. Most security work at the entry level leads to boredom, which of course is my prime ally. For many in the ranks, a shift, especially third shift, becomes something to tolerate. To endure a shift, sleeping, goofing off, watching TV, or sneaking off premises to obtain food or cigarettes all become ways to beat the boredom demon.

Having clear objectives for the security staff makes the job useful in fighting people like myself. A security force may have the best manager, a remarkable investigator, and an excellent commanding officer for the uniformed staff, but those people, fortunately for me, can't always be at the facility. Much of the burden for protection falls on entry-level security personnel.

Security personnel equipped with clear instructions of what needs to be done on each shift will not have time for boredom. However, they should not be burdened with trifles either. If the choice is between assisting employees with car problems and protecting intellectual property worth millions, please have them out there helping to jump start cars or changing flats. Minor busy work for them makes my job easier. But, building in observational checkpoints into the daily routine generates headaches for me. Teach them to observe, then make sure they practice the art.

As far as observational practices go, here are my suggestions:

1. When officers conduct a patrol, have them complete a checklist form showing where, when, and what they checked. If there are particularly sensitive areas that require regular inspection, please include them on the form. Remember your officer's shadow appearing about the premises is my nemesis.

2. Have different patrol routes established, which will be used in the course of a shift. One route may take in safety inspection points such as sprinkler system pressure, alarm panel status, refrigerator temperatures, heating and air conditioning systems status, and boiler system pressures. Another patrol may go by all key computer systems areas like the operations center, server rooms, computer labs, printer areas, telecommunications rooms and closets, and media storage areas. Other patrols will include checking copying, faxing, and document preparation areas and doing inspections for contraband. Just make sure any shift has a mix of the different patrols.

3. Specific things to look for on a patrol include:

   a. Inspect exterior doors and locks.

   b. Check all padlocks to critical areas. Verify the serial number of the locks and that the security officer's key works the lock.

   c. Check all internal doors to critical areas such as labs, computer rooms, document and computer media storage rooms, and executive offices.

   d. Test the functioning of any access controls such as card readers to internal areas.

   e. Walk through all areas where access to sensitive information is possible, whether that access involves keyboarding or touching paper documents. If workers hang around beyond their normal shift, politely check identification.

   f. Look for computer monitors or terminals left on and logged in, but the user has bolted from the vicinity. Document any such incidents with a report and secure the machine.

   g. Check file cabinets containing sensitive documents that are unlocked and unattended. Again, document the incident and secure the cabinets. (Develop a color-coded labeling scheme for such cabinets so that they can be spotted easily by security.)

   h. Locate any notebook, laptop, or palm-sized computers left in the open without a human partner. Document and secure the items. Leave a notice instructing the errant user where he or she can claim their electronic offspring.

i. Check all fax, copy machine areas, and shredder bin areas for sensitive documents or materials. If the machines have locking capabilities, insure that indeed they are locked or that someone removed the activation module or counter after use. Fax machines may need to be on 24 hours a day. If so, make sure the security officers know where to secure any nighttime faxes for retrieval by first shift. And, very important, security patrols should understand how to do a purge printout listing of the last ten to 20 faxes. That printout is something I always try to get from any of the fax machines, for it can contain some valuable intelligence. You want your security force to beat me to that information and get it secured. (If security finds sensitive documents at any of the above locations, have a procedure in place to secure them and to document the event.)

j. For any company, I recommend having a "clean desk" policy for when employees leave for the day. If your company doesn't have one, then it is only doing me a favor. Make sure security documents any violations of a clean desk policy and that they secure any sensitive materials. (There may be projects that require numerous documents being left out. If so, place those projects in a special room that workers lock at the end of each workday.)

k. Check behind the vending machines, in the refrigerators, above the ceiling tiles in the employee locker room, in the first aid kits, in the janitorial closets, and in the supply storage areas for contraband. Always keep your security force in the habit of looking in the crannies and crevices. It will keep them in form as good observers. And, it helps cast a broad security shadow on the plant. That shadow always makes me nervous. And, anyone that I bribe or hire gets scared.

l. Check loading docks and hallways for documents or computer media left there in error. (Again, have procedures to document the event and to remove the materials to a secure area.)

m. Have special projects for security patrols. One evening they may inspect, for example, all utility and telecommunications closets for signs of tampering, bugging, or break-in.

Most important, security managers should check on security officers to see that they conduct effective patrols. Planting test documents and simulated contraband periodically will keep them on their toes. If they do not find such test items, then they are not doing their jobs.

Other than completing checklists, security officers should have a secure way to report suspicious activities. Internal intelligence gathering needs to occur even at the entry-level. My hope is that any activities I conduct or my associates do go unnoticed while security officers watch TV, surf the Internet, play Solitaire, or engage in nonsecurity tasks assigned to them by the client. But, if you get them in the habit of reporting things that don't seem right, I'm going to run afoul of their vigilance.

Security officers are there to be "porcupines," sticking their barbs of curiosity into my activities. They prevent people like me from operating without a trace. Security can start coming after industrial spies by keeping track of the following:

1. People working unusual hours alone.
2. Employees found in areas not normally associated with their job.
3. Vendors found in areas not necessary for their work or in unauthorized areas.
4. Unusual events such as the diversion tactics we've discussed.
5. Employees sharing suspicions with security personnel.
6. Copy machines being used at unusual hours.
7. People who are not employees hanging around in the parking lot or who appear to be checking out the perimeter of the building.
8. People going through the trash or through items left on the loading dock.
9. Persons trying to gain access to critical areas without valid access cards.
10. Employees without badges or proper identification in the facility.
11. Employees with guests who have not been signed in and who do not possess visitors' badges.
12. Employees trying to remove computers, equipment, or sensitive records without the required property passes or documentation.
13. Employees or vendors bringing in outside computers, cameras, or computer media without appropriate written permission.
14. Any indication of computer "piggybacking." Someone using another user's terminal without doing his or her own login procedure.

15. Any indication of trying to by-pass physical security measures. These events range from rigging a door to stay open to disabling an access control device to turning off a video surveillance camera.

When these events occur, security officers should create a report that answers the five fundamental questions: Who, Where, When, Why, and How? The question, "Who is involved?" is the most critical. An environment where the security force regularly takes names and numbers lowers my comfort level considerably. I seek to be a will-o'-the-wisp and not someone identified in an intelligence report because I was doing something suspicious. When a target starts getting suspicious, I have to cut back on my activities to protect my cover.

Teach your security personnel to be nosy tactfully. They don't need to be overbearing to be effective. Just being watchful in a friendly way gets the job done. Good customer relations build alliances with the employees and visitors. When they are on security's side, it makes my job harder. They'll report things. Alienating employees with confrontational tactics only makes them hostile. They'll spend time rebelling, trying to hoodwink security. That is a much better atmosphere for me. Be suspicious with a smile.

Always make a show of your security staff inspecting video surveillance cameras, access card readers, locks, metal detectors, door alarms, and any other security technology they have in place. Let employees witness these inspections. I'll notice them too. They send me a message that your security program is watchful and probing. Probing is not something an industrial spy or her associates want.

Instill in your security force the need to keep focused. Prepare them for distractions, diversions, and the unreasonably demanding employee. Everyone on the force responding to one location when something out of the ordinary occurs doesn't accomplish much, except helping me out. Placating a demanding employee by deviating from security procedures opens the door for me. Sticking to the prime objective of protecting the company's assets has to be the overwhelming concern even if some people blow a fuse. Coverage needs to be maintained when a sprinkler head breaks or a door alarm starts blaring. The security force must see itself as more than a passive deterrent. When things get a little crazy, they must employ an active strategy to insure critical assets remain protected.

MORE TRAINING

To pick up on the strategy issue from our hypothetical spy, examining the nuts and bolts for developing an effective security policy appears in order. Ideally, the creation of a policy would contain the following steps:

1. Identify critical information assets that require constant protection. (This step is not a one-time action. It requires periodic reevaluation. And, management has the obligation to notify the security manager when the assets or their rankings change. Protecting everything with high-level resources is not feasible. So, management has to choose which assets will receive the greatest protection.)

2. Create rings of protection around those assets. These rings may involve a mix of Information Technology (IT) security, physical security, and alarm systems. Overlapping design becomes a critical factor. If one element fails, then another should be able to step in and protect the asset. So far, this approach constitutes traditional security doctrine. But, as indicated earlier in the text, static perimeter security, while not obsolete, faces shortcomings in a world of increasingly mobile information. Therefore, any defense plan also must accommodate the guarding of sensitive data when it passes outside of the traditional perimeter.

3. Devise smooth handoffs between different security elements. For example, IT personnel may have rock-solid network security procedures in place. However, once a user prints documents containing sensitive data, those documents need protection throughout their life cycle or until the value of the information expires. The IT staff needs to work with users to insure they transfer documents needing storage or destruction directly to the security staff or to a bonded service hired for those purposes. In the converse, if security normally posts an officer at the computer operations center's entrance, then an emergency transfer of that officer requires a backup plan to come into play. Someone from the IT staff needs to fill in at that post until the officer can return.

4. Security personnel, IT personnel, and users of sensitive information all need to understand their role in information security.

Basic counterespionage training for these individuals should include:

a. Defining industrial or corporate espionage.
b. Identifying the methods of attack commonly used:
   1. Diversion of security forces.
   2. Social engineering.
   3. Recruitment of employees.
   4. Penetration techniques such as piggybacking and working under a cover.
c. Explaining the life cycle of sensitive, proprietary information. Defining the difference between confidential information and trade secrets. (Confidential information contains data that is in the company's best interests not to be made public. Or, it may be information that the company has a legal obligation to keep secure, such as employee medical records for example. Trade secrets constitute an actual intellectual asset of the business. See Chapter 10 for a complete discussion.) Explain why these sensitive records and information must remain secure at their creation, during their use, in storage, and at their destruction. How users, IT personnel, and the security force all have a role to play in protection.
d. Giving suggestions to improve:
   1. Developing communications between different departments. (Who to call when something happens.)
   2. The handling and care of sensitive documents. (When to lock them up will depend upon the operational needs of the business.)
   3. The classifying of sensitive documents. (The categories of sensitive documents or files again will depend upon the nature of the company's business. Classification procedures will include color coding, using security headers and footers on documents, the stamping of documents with security labels, marking bulk documents, especially those for destruction, and whose responsibility is it to classify and mark sensitive documents.
   4. Identifying critical areas such as labs, computer operation centers, telecommunications rooms, mailrooms, printer and fax areas, and copy machine rooms. And discussing the vulnerabilities associated with those areas.

5. Discussing how to report suspicious events or activities.

Build into the protection system intelligence gathering operatives. Develop human assets to provide internal intelligence feedback. These operatives will come from among your security force and from regular workers willing to be eyes and ears. These individuals will receive advanced intelligence training. (More about this training in a minute.)

The security manager should create an information security master plan. But, any plan is useless without the involvement of and the consultation with the affected areas. Additionally, any plan becomes just a piece of paper if the affected parties fail to understand its elements and how to deal with violations. Finally, without trained informants, the plan remains deaf, dumb, and blind. No alert system exists to signal the security management team of danger on the horizon. These informants will refrain from being tattletales and purveyors of gossip. Professionally trained to gather mission-critical intelligence, they try to stop information attacks against the company before those attempts become big problems.

Informants, recruited from the security force and from the ranks of regular employees, create additional collision points between a spy or his associate and the security system. Threats, hopefully, will emerge on the radar sooner. Cramping the spy's working space is the goal.

Advanced training, beyond the basics offered to most employees, provides an inner council for the security manager. Niccolo Machiavelli comments in his book, *The Prince,* that a leader should engage in "choosing the wise men of his state and granting only to them the freedom to tell the truth." As we observed in Chapter 6, the currents and streams of power with the twenty-first century corporation can be more treacherous than a storm surf; security has to know what is going on. The security manager seeks the power of inside knowledge not for self-aggrandizement or to establish a private fiefdom. Rather, internal intelligence gathering, if done with restraint and wisdom, serves to protect the client and to safeguard that precious commodity, intellectual capital.

Selecting men and women for the internal intelligence mission requires finding persons of character. They must be stable individuals possessed with a respect for the rights of others. Moved by curiosity, they should look for "things that do not seem right." But, tempering their observations, when legal requirements dictate that they do so, is a necessary part of their job. They respect boundaries for action. They do not cross the line by being invasive when not permitted by law. Yet, they do not hesitate to be investigative when the situation calls for it. These individuals report timely, completely, and fairly, when events dictate, but they can also keep their mouths shut. Braggarts and gossips are not wanted.

As far as investigating employees by informants or by security staff is concerned, the watchword has to be avoiding any invasive actions. Employees have privacy rights, and violating them can bring serious civil penalties upon the company. Always consult legal counsel before drafting guidelines for internal investigations, which your company should have in place prior to instituting internal intelligence operations.

Internal informants may be employees of tenure or persons new to the company's work force. Again, character is the determining factor. Judge that character by job performance, interviews with the employee, and by interviews with managers and co-workers. And, of course, the employee must be able and willing to carry out intelligence gathering in addition to their regular job duties.

The advanced training concentrates on creating an intelligence product, whether written or oral, that is complete and actionable. Actionable reports provide answers as to what is going on, how often, and who is involved. Complete details are necessary.

John Cripenson, our fictional employee, may be acting suspiciously by working alone after hours. However, the details concerning when this practice started, and the subsequent dates and times involved, helps the security team to decide if the suspicion has substance. Since John is an exempt employee, he does not receive overtime pay, so he probably isn't working to earn extra money, at least from the company's payroll that is. Checking with his supervisor will reveal whether John's boss is aware of the practice and if a legitimate business reason requires the extra hours. This background intelligence gathering is something an employee informant can do by casual conversation on a low-key level. Informants training should cover developing information through informal means in nonthreatening ways.

Earlier in the chapter, we discussed suspicious activities. In advanced training, these activities need additional emphasis as far as keeping a watchful eye on them, but being able to cross-reference these events against other activity becomes critical. Looking for a cause and effect relationship between events defines the adept intelligence gatherer. Generating a field intelligence report that John works excessive overtime alone is praiseworthy. Tying that activity to sensitive documents suddenly appearing misfiled, or being left out at a copying station, to John's behavior produces actionable intelligence.

Being able to detect patterns amid multiple, diverse events requires teaching some analytical tools and skills. Index cards are an old stand-by for cross-referencing incident and intelligence reports. Creating an intelligence database using Microsoft's Access® or Excel® works quite well in a medium-sized company. In larger operations, an intelligence analytical tool like CaseRunner® may bring to the surface complex patterns of industrial espionage activity. A database of criminal incidents and field intelligence reports enables intelligence gatherers to focus in on areas or sectors of probable espionage activity. In the database have fields organized so the staff can search by name, location, date, time and incident type. (See Table 8-1.) A tool like CaseRunner goes a step further by tying together dissimilar evidence such as Web sites, photographs, paper documents, public records, computer files, personnel records, and online databases. The tool produces analytical reports, link charts, and can do searches by name, event, license plate number, and so on. (See Table 8-2.)

Table 8-2 interrelates dissimilar data. The car observed in the parking lot on several late night occasions matches by license plate against a known associate of John Cripenson, Carl Liefer. Liefer had registered as a daytime visitor of Cripenson a few weeks ago and security noted his license plate number on the registration form. Security entered the form into the security database along with property passes, incident reports, and field intelligence reports. In this case, the external patrol officer thought the car was suspicious, so he created a field intelligence report. When Cripenson's extra hours aroused suspicion, that information entered the database via an incident report. Since Cripenson's manager could neither verify nor question the validity of the extra hours, using the analytical tool security looked for other suspicious events during the same time period. Two events came up. First, Liefer's car in the parking lot produced a license plate. That plate in an ancillary search produced the link to Cripenson. And second, misfiled sensitive documents, according to an incident report, were located on two occasions the day after John Cripenson had been working late. John would not have been using these documents in his normal work.

Although an informant should not become a full-blown intelligence analyst, knowing enough about analysis will help focus an investiga-

Table 8-1.
INTELLIGENCE DATABASE EXAMPLE

Source	Name	Date	Time	Type	Location
Patrol 2nd Shift	John Cripenson	2-14-02	10:00 p.m.	Working late	Marketing
Patrol 2nd Shift	Vehicle XPP-555	2-14-02	10:30 p.m.	Unknown vehicle	K-5 Parking Lot
Patrol 3rd Shift	Marketing Documents	2-15-02	7:00 a.m.	Unsecured documents	Copy Room #3
Patrol 2nd Shift	John Cripenson	2-15-02	11:05 p.m.	Working late	Marketing

tion. Pattern recognition becomes an important skill for them to learn. Ideally, in larger companies, the security force will have an intelligence analyst on staff to advise the security staff and informants. The analyst will sift through large amounts of data and identify issues for additional investigation. But, the informants will have enough experience working with the intelligence database and the analytical tools themselves to recognize relationships between suspicious events. They can draw links and follow leads.

Industrial espionage is a process. An informant needs to understand the steps in that process. By understanding the process, an informant will recognize good interception points to catch the players. Those steps are:

1. *Initial Research.* Learning about the target from open sources to determine the best way to conduct the espionage campaign. (At this point in the cycle, an informant may observe an employee or a vendor trying to acquire information about areas in the company outside of their area of responsibility.)

2. *Penetration or Recruitment.* The spy penetrates the target or finds someone internal to acquire the information. (Signs of penetration range from evidence of a break-in to discovering people in unauthorized areas. Signs of recruitment may include sudden reversals of fortune in finances or in the employee's social life.)

3. *Compromising Sensitive Information.* The actual theft of information occurs. (The telltale signs include the hacking of and penetrations of IT systems, the temporary removal of documents, the outright theft of documents, and the less than clandestine copying of sen-

Table 8-2.
INTEGRATING INTELLIGENCE DATA

Source	Association	Name	Date	Location	Event	Other Links
Patrol 2nd Shift	Vehicle XPP-555		02-14-02	Unknown Vehicle	K-5 Parking Lot	Carl Liefer
Motor Vehicle Department	Plate XPP-555	Carl Liefer	02-15-02	K-5 Parking Lot	Run Plate	John Cripenson
Visitor Pass	John Cripenson	Carl Liefer	01-20-02	Office	Visit to John Cripenson	Plate XPP-555
Patrol 3rd Shift	Marketing Documents		02-15-02	Unsecured documents	Copy Room #3	John Cripenson
Patrol 2nd Shift	John Cripenson		02-14-02	Working late	Marketing	Vehicle XPP-555
Secretary of State Corporations	John Cripenson	ABC Investment Company	06-13-02	Austin, Texas	John is VP in company	Liefer is Treasurer in company

sitive documents. Spies or compromised employees sometimes get sloppy and leave documents out. Or, the security force can interrupt them.)

4. *Endgame.* The spy turns over the product to his or her client. The espionage operation normally comes to an end. (Again the spy or her associates can get careless here. They may not terminate the mission smoothly by neglecting to erase all the paper and electronic trails behind them. The goal of the internal intelligence program to prevent them from coming in and out cleanly. Hopefully, parts of the counterintelligence effort will stick to them, providing clues for later investigation.)

5. *Disclosure.* The sensitive proprietary data finally enters the marketplace. Or, confidential data becomes public. (This may be the first time that the target realizes that it is a victim of industrial espionage.)

An informant's training needs to point out that most likely they will catch an industrial espionage case well past the first step. Usually, they encounter bits and pieces in the "Endgame" phase. The ability to go back in time and reconstruct past events builds a case. The daily intelligence collection efforts, which create paper trails in incident reports, field intelligence reports, and the like, enable reconstruction and analysis to take place.

Finally, informants should learn the elements of investigating incidents beyond the initial intake of case facts. Rarely will the fruits of industrial espionage shout at them. Instead, security will encounter small pieces of evidence that could suggest something major or something of little consequence to the espionage picture. Sorting out the different interpretations to an evidence fragment is a central part of counterintelligence work.

For example, a security officer on patrol finds a floppy disk in the parking lot. The disk has no label. She takes the disk inside and examines its contents on a computer. Marketing plans are on the disk. What further action should take place? Perhaps, an employee dropped the disk when fumbling for her car keys. Maybe this person did not realize that the floppy contained a sensitive file.

An investigation of the "dropped floppy" case would require the following:

1. Determine the chain of events that allowed the asset to leave the secured premises. Why was the floppy not labeled? Who copied the file onto the disk? Why weren't chain of custody measures effective in preventing the copying? Concentrate on the physical path the data and the floppy took within the company. The manufacturer and type of disk may provide clues as to which department first used the floppy. Examining the disk with a hex editor may reveal deleted files that give a clue as to the previous handlers or users.

2. If you narrow the disk's source to a particular department, the informant in that area should be able to do low-key peer interviews to find out how the file was copied.

3. If the investigation rules out an accidental cause, security may want to draft a list of suspects. These individuals are persons with direct access to the sensitive data. If other evidence indicates that they may have had an opportunity to piggyback on someone else's privileges, then include them as a suspect too.

4. The security manager should turn the matter over to the security investigator to develop chronological tie-ins for the suspects and any background investigations needed on those suspects. (See Chapter 10, "An Investigative Checklist.")

DISCUSSION

1. Debate the ethics of gathering intelligence internally against industrial espionage. What activities would be permissible? Under what circumstances would you do those activities? When would you search an employee's desk, office, locker, computer, or even a motor vehicle?

2. Research on the Internet the legalities of doing the above. (See the Chapter Notes for some suggestions on Web sites to visit.)

3. Why is an intelligence database important to have in a larger company? Incident and intelligence report from security officers would go into the database. What other kinds of information should go into the database?

4. If sensitive data presently in paper form or on storage media originated on the IT system, why is it important to trace its path all

the way through the documentary system back into the IT system? How would an IT expert or a computer forensics professional assist in the effort?

5. Why is it better to try to prove someone innocent of industrial espionage involvement rather than assume that person guilty at the investigation's beginning? Stay probing after the facts; do not pursue people unless the facts lead you there. Comment on these assertions and explain how they affect privacy issues.

6. Why should counterespionage training be two-tiered? (Most employees would receive basic training, while advanced training would be for selected security personnel and for informants.)

Chapter 9

EXTERNAL INTELLIGENCE

We work for an illusion. Our client, especially if a large company or organization, does not dwell in the fixed, static images of the past. Perhaps, in the middle of the twentieth century, where everything fit into the nice, neat boxes of industrial organization, the static conception had some validity. Companies tended to do what they had done in the past, staying within their particular lines of commerce or manufacture. In the twenty-first century, constant flux and change prevail. A static vision beckons dangerous misconceptions. Your trusted boss may not be your boss tomorrow. Alliances within and outside of a company shift like pebbles on the beach. The list of information assets needing protection will not remain fixed, etched in some stone monument in the executive suite.

Today's security professional has to think about disciplines outside of security. Coursework in security principles, physical measures, criminal investigation techniques, and legal issues all form a useful foundation. Once on the job, however, understanding the business environment of the client often overshadows any mere technical security knowledge. The people the security professional works for will be preoccupied with business concerns, not security issues. To maintain the ear of management, the security professional studies the business as a business not just as a "protectee." Savvy and diligence dictate that the security professional quietly learn the business and the industry. Assessing the strengths and weaknesses of the company in the business arena aids in identifying both internal and external threats.

A security manager will acquire knowledge about the company from:

A. The Annual Report
B. Internal Company Publications

C. News Accounts
D. Industry Journals and Trade Magazines
E. Industry Analyst Reports on the Company
F. Comparisons Made in the Press with Competitors
G. Attendance at Business Conferences and Meeting
H. Attendance at Company Meetings

This information provides the necessary background to judge how events in the business arena will impact the company's operations. Such background data will help in drafting a vulnerability matrix. Such a tool prevents the security manager from being taken by surprise.

Staying in tune with the business environment will help security anticipate economic challenges that could impact security operations. This insight assists in developing budgets and in allocating resources to address probable threats. The vulnerability matrix identifies areas where information thieves may strike. If the company possesses a clear technology lead in certain sectors, the matrix can identify the nature and possible sources of attack. (See Table 9-1.)

Where the technological lead is commanding such as against Big Agriscience, Inc., the motivation for industrial espionage increases. However, the mere existence of a technological lead does not mean that a competitor's only option will be industrial espionage. Technologically superior products do not always triumph in commerce. A competitor may rely on better marketing, sales, and financial strategies to penetrate the marketplace, undermining the technological advantage. Learning a competitor's capabilities in other areas becomes very important. Competitive intelligence goes hand-in-hand with security analysis. But, most important, what becomes paramount is learning a competitor's intentions. In discovering a competitor's intentions, however, the pursuit raises the greatest paradox and dilemma for security professionals.

The security professional seeks to protect the client against industrial espionage. In order to accomplish that mission, what is permissible in learning about the intentions of a competitor? To make sure that others are not stealing secrets from the client, does the security manager have to be a spymaster, a modern day Walsingham? Obviously, spying in government service for the United States does not carry the same ethical dilemma. The safety of every man, woman, child in our nation may depend upon what our intelligence services learn.

Table 9-1.
VULNERABILITY MATRIX EXAMPLE

Factor	Source	Level	Department(s) Affected	Business Line	Security Impact
Technology Lead	"Big Agriscience Falls Behind" *New York Times* 3/8/02	Moderate Concern	Plant Genetics Research	Seeds	Monitor News Coverage
Parity	GenCrop (from analyst's report)	Low	Plant Genetics Research	Seeds	Low
Foreign Power	Graduate student at a West Coast university tried to sell research to a company in Europe *LA Times* 3/19/02	Significant Threat	Pharmaceuticals	Medicines: Anti-viral	Tighten controls on proprietary data in independent lab

But, industrial espionage is stealing, not military self-defense. The right of businesses to engage countermeasures against this theft remains unquestioned. Businesses also have the right to impede legal business intelligence efforts through cloaking operations, disinformation, or by obscuring information as long as such efforts are not illegal.

The degree to which a business may collect information about its competitors has definite ethical limits. (Legal limits we will discuss in Chapter 10.) Information about a competitor available in the public sector is permissible for your client's use. Viewing a competitor's facilities or operations from a place where the public is permitted also falls within what is acceptable. Few experts in business ethics would quibble with these assertions. At the other end of the spectrum, obvious illegal acts such as burglary, criminal trespass, commercial bribery, or extortion would hardly receive approval by reasonable business people.

The gray area emerges when interviewing people. Interviewees may be current employees, former employees, suppliers, vendors, customers, and others associated with the competitor. Such interviews, as long as they are conducted without fraud or misrepresentation, and as long as the interviewer identifies whom their client or employer is, probably are ethical. The Web site for the Society of Competitive Intelligence Professionals (SCIP) at http://www.scip.org offers additional information on this issue.

This text holds that a client may conduct business intelligence gathering in a reasonably ethical manner against competitors. (The only proviso is that the target of such intelligence operations has no obligation to make it easy for the business intelligence researcher.) Business intelligence emerges as one component in an overall intelligence strategy to protect the client's position in the marketplace. Without active intelligence operations in place, any security effort gropes about blind in an environment of constant flux.

Before moving on with discussing the overall external intelligence effort, a brief talk about spying on spies is in order. What are the constraints in this area? How ethical does one have to be in dealing with an industrial spy? Causing physical harm or intentionally exposing the spy to physical danger is out of the question. The same goes for breaking into the spy's automobile or home, and certainly wiretapping is taboo. In other words do not break the law to catch a thief. (If your investigation reaches the point where an external search of a spy's premises or electronic eavesdropping becomes warranted, get law enforcement involved. They can obtain the necessary search warrants or court orders.) Yet, lying to the information thief, misdirecting his or her efforts, cloaking company operations, misrepresenting facts to the spy, which he or she may access, and leading the culprit into a legal trap are all permissible, provided they remain within the bounds of the law. Trickery that allows the spy to follow his or her own scheme usually is legal.

BUILDING INTELLIGENCE RESOURCES

An initial step involves adding to your vulnerability matrix social, political, and economic factors (S/P/E). A "what-if" analysis, this technique uses a brief scenario. For example, a change in governmental regulations may alter or harm Scientific Fish Proteins, Inc.'s parity with your research program. In the case of new permit requirements, your company may meet the new specifications, but Scientific Fish Proteins cannot satisfy the new strictures in the near future. The competitive parity suddenly disappears. (See Table 9-2.)

Rising public opposition to genetic research heightens the chance for increased monitoring or even spying on your operations by activist groups. This action raises the issue of politically inspired industrial espionage. Most of the industrial spying we've discussed has been financially motivated. Politically motivated spying carries new challenges. First, radical lifestyle and financial changes may not occur in an employee spying for a cause. So, investigating this flavor of industrial espionage may be more difficult. Second, an employee's politics, much like their religious beliefs, are their own affair, falling under First Amendment protection. As long as the employee does not cause disruptions at work, investigating their political affiliations is "off limits."

Finally, the goal of politically motivated intelligence gathering is to expose "corporate wrongdoing." In the company's eyes, someone is stealing proprietary information. From the activist's perspective the company's unethical or illegal conduct finally receives the light of day. When the company tries to block these attempts, allegations of obstruction of justice may surface. Responding to political industrial espionage requires setting limits. The company has to respond of course, but it should refrain from overreacting. Avoid any appearance of being on a

Table 9-2.
S/P/E FACTORS (EXAMPLE)

Factor	Company	Social Impact	Political Impact	Economic Impact	Security Impact
New Federal Regulation	Scientific Fish Proteins	N/A	N/A	Competitor has problems raising new capital, may not be able to meet new regulations. *Washington Post* 4-11/02	Monitor News Accounts
Documents from a genetics lab in Sweden posted on the Internet 4-25-02	Affects entire Biotechnology Industry	Rising concern by public may encourage insiders to steal information.	Increasing activism, may hinder permit approvals for research. May lead to internal information theft.	Possible compromise of proprietary data.	Evaluate internal controls on highly sensitive documents in research center.

"witch hunt." Industrial espionage remains a crime regardless of the motivations of the perpetrators. Good, solid investigative methods, as laid out in Chapter 10, will establish any wrongdoing by overly zealous activists. If adequate internal intelligence systems are in place, suspicious activity will come to security's attention. The company just needs to be sure that by investigating that activity it does not trample on the civil liberties of employees.

If a vulnerability assessment indicates that politically-based spying is a real threat, then undertake strong compartmentalization of sensitive information. Projects with real target potential should come under strict need-to-know access rules. A rigorous S/P/E analysis can forecast heightened political and social activity against the client. It remains a tool for proactive, outward-looking responses to external attacks.

S/P/E scenarios help visualize developments in the outside world that alter the company's vulnerabilities. (An example is available in Table 9-3.) Usually, crafting the scenarios will not require creating a special unit. The Business Intelligence (BI) unit within the company should be able to incorporate this function within their regular operations.

The BI unit probably would not fall under the security department. Providing competitive intelligence to the company's operating units is their prime mission. Main sources of information to the BI unit include:

1. Access to major databases such as Dialog, Profound, and Lexis-Nexis.
2. Major Industry Trade Journals and magazines.
3. S/P/E sources such as *The New York Times, The Washington Post, The Los Angeles Times, Business Week,* and *The Economist.*
4. Field intelligence reports from the sales force, marketing, and the technical staff.
5. Interviews with key persons in the industry.
6. Analyst's reports.

At first look, the work of the BI unit may seem slightly alien to what security does. Instead, view the BI unit as a direct supplement to security's own knowledge base. Not only does the unit aid in interpreting S/P/E trends, but it also supplies all the primary executives within the company a continuous review of the company's competitive position.

Table 9-3.
SCENARIOS (EXAMPLE)

Scenario	Security Impact	Business Impact	Countermeasures Needed	Probability Factor
A severe contraction in venture capital for biotechnology firms starts a fallout of the less stable companies.	Companies move from a long-term focus to short-term sales in order to generate cash. The desperation may lead to corporate spying.	Firms have to shift from an investor orientation to getting paying customers. Customer lists and databases could become a valuable commodity. Also, research data on products nearly ready for market release becomes highly valuable.	1. Review security procedures on customer lists and databases. 2. Check information security procedures on products nearing market release.	The industry press considers a contraction to be a probable event unless the economy improves early next year.
Military action in the Middle East involves the release of biological warfare agents with significant civilian casualties.	Depending upon the tone of public reaction, security may have to prepare for militant extremist activity. Politically motivated employees may leak information or steal proprietary documents.	The public may not be able to differentiate between the military and civilian uses of biotechnology. Biotechnology businesses may experience boycotts, domestic terrorism, and corporate spying.	1. Plans for the cloaking of operations and critical locations should be on the drawing board. 2. Need-to-know requirements should be tightened.	The military press considers this event to be very probable in the next two years. Domestic public reaction remains an unknown factor.

As we indicated previously, knowing where the company stands in the market provides insight on probable threats.

Fostering a working relationship with the BI unit may require some lobbying by the security manager. Yet, the demands of the twenty-first century business environment require the pooling and sharing of information. Building alliances minimizes the isolation of diverse information resources within the company. Mutual respect and understanding leads to sharing critical intelligence. The goal of security must be to increase the inflow of intelligence and to decrease unauthorized information outflow. A BI unit and the security department are in a position to share resources such as electronic databases and to minimize costs. Each department will put the information to different uses, but they should also develop a dialogue on their different perspectives.

The security manager should consider creating an Economic Espionage Unit (EEU). This unit would be a twin to the BI unit. However, it functions like a criminal intelligence unit. Staffed by an intelligence analyst, an investigator, and a database administrator, the unit acts as a clearinghouse for internal intelligence, maintaining the security database. Yet, the unit also ventures out into the world to gather external intelligence.

Typical external sources for the EEU would include the following:

1. Scanning for information on the Internet about the company. This data comes from a wide range of sites: hacker sites, newsgroups, business sites, political activist pages, warez pirated software sites, and those industry-related Web sites. Gaining a broad view of what is being said about the company online becomes the prime goal. This focused surfing technique also picks up actionable intelligence. A hacker may be passing on a tip about a flaw that they've found in the company's security defenses.
2. Reviewing competitor actions and developments. (Supplied by BI unit.)
3. Networking with other security professionals in the private and public sectors. This interaction identifies emerging information security threats.
4. Monitoring the major publications in the security field for emerging threats and trends. Also, the unit studies incidents involving industrial espionage.

5. Checking the general press for cases involving industrial espionage. As a supplement to this review, the unit runs inquiries on say LexisNexis based upon probable threats. For example, "Industrial Espionage- Plant Genetics" produces cases, stories, or incidents relevant to that area of biotechnology. Such research may provide sufficient details to assist in investigating a case or to prevent a similar incident from occurring. Again, this database can be a shared resource between the EEU and the BI units.

6. Following industrial espionage investigations when the trail of evidence leads outside of the company's walls. Such an outreach may involve background investigations of suspects and coordination with law enforcement.

7. Interrogating the company's security incident database looking for connections between external events and internal incidents. (Both internal incidents and external events, which could have a security impact, go into the incident database.) An internal pattern of industrial espionage may not become apparent unless correlated against external events. Detecting subtle patterns often requires first knowing what to look for. Knowledge of criminal activity elsewhere enables the latent to become visible in your backyard. (See Table 9-4.)

The security manager should regularly receive the BI unit's intelligence product like other leaders in the company. This information should be correlated with the product from the EEU. Ideally, the BI and EEU units will share information based upon common interests. Members of the respective units will possess the appropriate security background checks. They understand that their respective missions are both highly sensitive and confidential. An area of possible joint operations is in monitoring "emerging technologies."

Emerging technologies represent innovations that alter the company's competitive environment. New methods of manufacture render existing methods obsolete. From a business standpoint, constant surveillance for technological revolutions generates a competitive edge. With enough advance notice, relatively smooth strategic shifts are possible. Changing production methods, research efforts, marketing programs, and raising the capital necessary for it all become feasible when the company has its periscope above the surface to see what is going on.

Table 9-4.
INTERNAL AND EXTERNAL SOURCES (EXAMPLE)

Source	Date	Time	Location	Description	Cross-reference to run on database
Patrol 3rd Shift	06-19-02	0100	Genetics Lab	Unlocked Security Cabinet holding stem cell agents; possibly agents missing.	Stem cell bonding agents to glue
Austin American-Statesman, August 5, 2002	08-05-02		University of California, Davis	Alleged theft of stem cell glue	Stem cell
LexisNexis Search	08-06-02	0900	2 hits in our state—Texas	11 hits on database: 4 articles genetics lab thefts, 3 articles stem cell materials-theft, 4 articles on biotechnology-thefts of supplies.	Genetics lab thefts, stem cell materials-thefts, biotechnology-thefts of supplies

The resources for monitoring emerging technologies are those used by the BI unit as discussed above. And, the science and technical sources discussed in Chapter 2 will supplement the research effort. The methodology involves not so much new sources as mining the information base for new trends and for shifts in technology. When the security staff comes across references to new technologies relevant to the company, they should pass on the data to the BI unit. They act like an intelligence gatherer similar to what sales, marketing, or technical staff does in their daily work.

No one disputes the eventual obsolescence of manufacturing facilities. Companies constantly modernize their equipment to keep up with a changing competitive environment. In the realm of security, however, how often is the obsolescence of security systems discussed? Many high-tech facilities receive current security technology when they initially open their doors. But, very often the equipment does not receive adequate maintenance, and management fails to keep it up to date. Many video surveillance systems, radio communications equipment, and alarm systems function poorly, partially, or not at all. In fact, many facilities operate with aged systems in need of replacement, but are retained with patchwork repairs. Some facilities engaged in high-tech production have a guard force in place whose equipment and techniques Allan Pinkerton would have no problem recognizing. Gathering intelligence on the current abilities of security systems needs to be a part of the EEU's mission. Comparing current practice against the existing security technology in place is a prime directive for the security manager. Maintaining a capital budget to upgrade defenses is a mandatory practice, not a luxury.

The BI unit should also identify technological changes requiring new security measures. Imagine the head start computer security would have had if business intelligence concentrated on those issues in the early 1990s. The current move to wireless and increasingly mobile computing creates a whole new realm of security risks. This area needs a great deal of intelligence focus and analysis. Every new technology brings new security risks. Very often, the criminals will be well ahead of us. They will know all the cracks and dents in the armor before we even think about them. Who thought much about identity theft a few years ago? In the security field we need to be much more anticipatory, or we will always be playing "catch up." Effective use of BI and EEU units can make a big step toward closing that gap.

Integration of intelligence from diverse sources enables the modern corporation to stay ahead of industrial espionage. Recognizing this fact and implementing it, however, become entirely two different matters. Many factors work against a security manager making intelligence gathering an integral part of the security plan:

1. In many companies resources allocated to the security department remain limited. Funding is not proportional to the risks the company faces.
2. Entry-level personnel to the security department have high turnover rates due to low pay and limited educational backgrounds. Training programs for them rarely go beyond the basic patrol duties. Expanding their role draws skepticism, often deemed not worth the effort.
3. Managers often view Security departments as being a necessary evil. Security operations draw resources and do not produce toward the bottom line. They are not perceived as centers of creativity within a company.
4. The industrial espionage threat remains below the radar for most upper echelon managers. Making the threat a reality frequently is a hard sell.
5. Looking outside the company to gather intelligence is unsettling for some managers. Security should just pay attention to what is happening within the four walls, the thinking goes.

These are harsh realities, perceptions that are not going to disappear any time soon. But somehow, the security manager has to overcome them and cultivate new perceptions. Transformation requires creativity and some sales skills. And obviously, this text delineates the full-blown, ultimate intelligence plan. (Isn't that always what texts do? They give the ideal, while the reality is always different. All I can say is treat it like a blueprint; you are free to make alterations depending upon your circumstances.) So start with simple intelligence methods and build them into your organization. From the internal side, getting your security force to report in a systematic way unusual or suspicious activity can get the ball rolling. On the external side, networking with other security professionals, law enforcement, and reading security publications is a good start.

The constant refrain I hear from workers in all the differing fields of work, not just security, is "there's no time for creativity." Ralph Waldo

Emerson observed in his landmark essay, "Self-Reliance," that daily existence works against creativity and lures us into mediocrity. "At times the whole world seems to be in conspiracy to importune you with emphatic trifles." As a security professional develop a reputation as a creative manager. Work for innovative solutions to everyday security problems and in servicing your customer. Constantly solicit ideas from others whether they wear a white collar (Or, is it executive casual today?), a blue collar, or no collar. To get upper management's attention, always speak in terms of dollars: what security measures can save the company and what a lack of measures may cost the business.

DISCUSSION

1. Describe ways that a corporate BI unit and an EEU can coexist peacefully, work jointly as the need arises, and share resources.
2. Explain how learning about industrial espionage cases at other companies will help fight industrial espionage within your business.
3. Identify ways a security manager builds alliances with other departments within the company.
4. What daily activities can a security professional do to be creative on his or her job? Being creative does not equate with being dramatic; doing little things can add up. Be specific.

Chapter 10

INVESTIGATING CASES

In the fight against industrial espionage, the security specialist employs good intelligence gathering and effective investigative methods as the fundamental weapons. Effective investigation leads to punishment for industrial spies. Punishment can be a viable deterrent. Unlike common-law crimes though, trade secret theft is a technical crime that requires more than just catching the offender. The perpetrator may argue that the information taken fails to meet the legal standard of what constitutes a trade secret. Or, oddly enough, that the information doesn't have significant value.

The concept of trade secrets existed in colonial America. Apprenticeship or indenture agreements to learn a trade prohibited the apprentice from revealing the master's secrets of his trade. The language of a Massachusetts Bay Colony indenture agreement from 1748 reads, ". . . his said Master and Mistress well and faithfully shall Serve, their secrets he shall keep close. . . ." However, heavyweight legal protections for trade secrets in the criminal law didn't arise in America until the twentieth century. The definition of this crime depends upon the crafted language of state and federal statutes. Very specific technical requirements have to be met for a successful prosecution. Most jurors know a common-law crime when they see the evidence for it. For them to understand this crime often requires painstaking investigation.

Learning the requirements for investigating an industrial espionage case yields security benefits beyond successful prosecutions. A company needs to undertake certain steps and safeguards with the handling of trade secrets prior to a theft. Otherwise, a company may not have any criminal or civil remedies. Security professionals definitely need to know these rules.

The law recognizes four major types of intellectual property: patents, copyrights, trademarks, and trade secrets. Infringements of copyrights and trademarks are not within the scope of this book. We discussed patent infringement in Chapter 6. When we speak of industrial espionage in this chapter, we are talking about trade secret theft. As we indicated before, not everything a company wants to keep confidential is a trade secret. Certain financial and operational information deserves protection by the security team, but its compromise may not result in an actionable remedy under the law.

While many states have statutes on industrial espionage and on trade secret theft, our focus will be on the federal statute, the *Economic Espionage Act of 1996* (Title 18, U.S. Code, Chapter 90, Sections 1831-1839.) The act, while far from encompassing every nuance of the legal issues, does provide an excellent overview of the fundamental concepts. It serves as a good checklist or benchmark for an investigator; however, our discussion is not intended to replace the guidance of competent legal counsel, so seek legal assistance when undertaking these complex investigations.

The act defines under American law what constitutes a "trade secret." "All forms of financial, business, scientific, technical, economic, or engineering information" come under the term's umbrella. At first glance, the definition seems overly broad. But, two important provisos exist. To qualify as a trade secret the owner must have taken "reasonable measures to keep such information secret." In other words, if the owner has acted in a sloppy or negligent manner and has not instituted reasonable safeguards to protect the secret, a secret in the law's eyes may not exist. What is "reasonable" depends upon court decisions in other cases and the presiding court's interpretation of those decisions. Reviewing the case law on this issue remains beyond the scope of this text. However, a security specialist must ask the critical question: "How would an independent security professional evaluate the measures taken by the company to safeguard the highly sensitive data?" A wronged business may claim a large loss due to trade secret theft. But, such a claim may go unheeded by the courts if the company never spent more than a pittance on protecting the information and failing to provide even minimal information security. (An important factor to argue when obtaining security budgets from upper management.)

The second proviso requires that "the information derives independent economic value, actual or potential, from not being generally known to, and not being readily ascertainable through proper means by the public." In everyday English, the trade secret can't be easily discoverable by the public. (If the secret gets published accidentally by the owner on the Internet, the trade secret no longer exists.) And, the secret's value arises from it not being known by the public. (The public not knowing can't be simply a nice advantage; the source of the secret's value must depend on that fact.)

Be confident of the fact that in any litigation, whether criminal or civil, the defense will argue, "My client didn't steal anything, but if he did, it wasn't a trade secret, and even if it was a 'secret,' it didn't have any value." Expect to get hammered on these points. Always investigate to prove up the legal status of the intellectual property as a trade secret.

Article I, Section 8, Clause 8 of the *United States Constitution* recognized the rights of intellectual property owners to have exclusive title to that property and to profit from that right. Under the *Constitution,* Congress has the power to grant patents and copyrights for limited periods of time. Once those periods expire, the intellectual property enters the public realm. The framers of the *Constitution* wanted to balance rewarding inventors, writers, and artists against insuring that mankind eventually has access to the property.

In recent years, Congress recognized that it was in the public's interest to grant trade secrets criminal law protection. American society without strong protection of these private rights could end up intellectually poor, literally starved for ideas, because those ideas were in someone else's hands.

Not all trade secret theft falls under the federal act. The act focuses on trade secrets targeted by foreign governments and on trade secrets for products already in interstate or foreign commerce. Under section 1831, the theft (or the obtaining by deception, fraud, or unauthorized access) of a trade secret benefits a foreign government, foreign instrumentality, or foreign agent, the act authorizes a fine of up to $500,000 or 15 years in prison, or both. The Act authorizes fines to $10,000,000 against organizations. Receiving stolen trade secrets or conspiring to steal them also come under the Act. (A foreign agent works on behalf of a foreign government. A foreign instrumentality is "substantially owned, controlled, sponsored, commanded, managed, or dominated by a foreign government.")

Under section 1832, if a trade secret's product is in interstate commerce or foreign commerce, any party can be held responsible for its theft. The same protections against deception, fraud, unauthorized access, receiving, buying, and conspiring to steal apply. The penalties for violations under this section are a fine and up to ten (10) years in prison. Organizations may receive fines up to $5,000,000.

The absence of a foreign power negates coverage. And, the lack of interstate or international commerce prevents federal involvement. So, a trade secret theft would not fall under the federal statutes. However, it still may be a violation of the state's industrial espionage or trade secrets statute. Check with legal counsel if your situation points away from the federal act.

AN INVESTIGATIVE CHECKLIST

With some law under our belt, let us look at the key points in an I.E. investigation. (See also Figure 10-1.)

1. Identify evidence that someone stole or converted by deception or fraud a trade secret. Evidence of unauthorized access to a secure computer system would also be acceptable.
2. Establish that the object of the crime was a trade secret.
3. Develop evidence of a foreign government's involvement in the theft.
4. In the alternative, establish evidence of a product in interstate or foreign commerce.
5. Identify the parties responsible for the crime.
6. Establish the value of the trade secret. And, establish the value of the loss caused by the trade secret's theft.

Item one tells the judge and the jury how the crime occurred. The event made the basis of the crime required intent. Any criminal actor must have knowingly or intentionally sought to cause economic injury by stealing the trade secret. The accidental removal of a trade secret from the owner's premises would not be a crime. For example, I take a floppy disk home not knowing it has a proprietary marketing plan on the disk. So, proving intent is vital to a case.

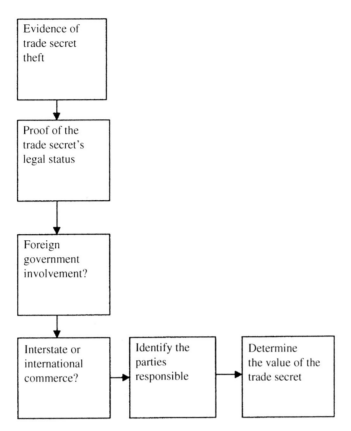

Figure 10-1. Steps in a Trade Secret Theft Case

The offender's actions generally prove intent. He or she commits a common-law crime to enter the premises such as burglary, the theft of an access card, or the stealing or the forging of an identity badge. The spy may violate state or federal computer crime laws to gain illegal entry to a computer or network.

The difficult area on the intent issue is when an employee has normal, regular authorization to a trade secret. Simply catching them with the floppy in the parking lot doesn't establish a criminal act. They can attribute it to an error or an oversight. You have to catch them passing the intelligence product to their handler or client. Or, an extensive background investigation showing lifestyle or income changes the subject can't explain has strong circumstantial clout. Sometimes, setting bait for a rogue employee, in the style of Clifford Stoll's *The Cuckoo's Egg*, will be a viable technique. (See Chapter 4.) The employee needs to cross the line and access information he or she had no authorization to see, never mind remove. The evidence on intent must be unambiguous. Otherwise, a jury may give the perpetrator the benefit of reasonable doubt.

Defense counsel in a trade secret case will try to show the property stolen was not a trade secret. In assisting in the prosecution of the case, the company will be asked to provide evidence that the object stolen meets the legal definition. Any investigation should assemble evidence of the steps the business took to protect the trade secret. The safeguards do not have to be superhuman, just what a reasonable businessperson would do. Obviously, having an information security plan in place with a reasonable amount of access enforcement will fill the bill here. The public must not have legal access to the information. What research will the defense counsel do in a trade secrets case? Remember that even unplanned, inadvertent Internet postings of proprietary data or the accidental release in print may cause the loss of trade secret protection.

Anticipate the defense counsel's online and print research. Never assume the impossibility of an accidental release. Always do a check on the Internet and in the technical press. Also, be on the lookout for publicly available information similar in content to the trade secret. Opposing counsel may use that information as evidence that the trade secret is public knowledge. Of any similarity to the trade secret may be minimal at best, but issues involving gray areas form the basis of most litigation.

Developing evidence of foreign government culpability will probably require law enforcement's involvement. The mere fact that the suspected spy is a foreign national does not make the case. Sometimes an arrest of the suspect will be necessary, and subsequent interrogation will uncover the foreign government's involvement. Evidence developed via wiretap orders or search warrants also build evidence of the relationship. Building a financial paper trail is another possibility, but this approach usually requires grand jury subpoenas or court orders. So, proving foreign involvement, unless the spy is very sloppy, generally falls to law enforcement.

Establishing interstate or foreign commerce prior to the trade secret's theft usually is a straightforward matter of documentary evidence. Invoices for sales to parties in their states or countries will meet the requirements of the federal statute. Provided these records are kept in the normal course of business, the custodian of those records can testify. Of course, the Marketing and Sales managers also may testify that the product dependent upon the trade secret was in interstate or international commerce. If the company has multiple products, the investigation focuses on the product derived from the trade secret and establishes that product is in the interstate or international commerce stream. If the product only has distribution in intrastate commerce, which is less and less likely in this Internet-based world, then the state statute would have to apply.

Identifying the party or parties responsible for industrial espionage has different approaches based upon the method of the theft. Theft of a trade secret by burglary would follow the normal investigative path of trying to develop as much forensic evidence as possible. Unfortunately, other investigative resources like confidential informants or "fences", such as pawnshops, aren't much help. Industrial spies usually do not run in those circles. Usually, stolen intellectual property does not trade on the streets.

Yet, making an internal theft look like a burglary could provide cover for an employee with access to the information. A burglary of intellectual property without prior knowledge of where to look for the information would be unlikely. If you have suspicions that the burglary may be a "red herring," begin to evaluate employees as suspects.

In cases where a common-law crime does not trigger the investigation, the investigator has to work back from the point of discovery. Discovery points include:

1. Other companies place into the marketplace products based upon your business' trade secret.
2. An audit trail on the IT system reveals unauthorized access to sensitive files.
3. Sensitive documents or media are found left outside of secure storage or in an unauthorized area.
4. Email, postings on an electronic bulletin board, or in a newsgroup make references to a theft via unauthorized access or to weaknesses in the company's security system.
5. An employee reports suspicious activity by a co-worker, a vendor, or a consultant.
6. An employee reports social engineering attempts on him or her.

7. A new contact that asks suspicious questions approaches an employee at a technical meeting.

Item one is not an enviable place to start an investigation. The damage occurred some time ago. At face value, no leads run from your company to the competitors. It may require civil suits or a criminal investigation by law enforcement to uncover connections. Checking the personnel records of employees who have left the company in the last year and who had possible access to the information may yield leads. Especially, if they now work for a competitor, always consider those persons as prime suspects.

Item two at least presents the possibility for a strong lead. The audit logs from the server on the network will reveal which user accessed the restricted file. With the assistance of the network manager, security charts the user's activity for the date in question. Was the user of record the actual person on the keyboard? Or, could this be a case of piggybacking? Perhaps, someone from outside the network penetrated the defenses and usurped a user's account. IT-based espionage generates stronger leads than you might think. Developing them often requires technical assistance and examination by computer forensics experts in addition to in-house network professionals. The questions technical and forensic examination often answers are:

A. When and from where the user account was accessed?
B. Are there changes in the pattern of usage on the computer at the time of the theft? (Did the user suddenly shift gears in his or her searching after a lull period?) A sudden change may indicate piggybacking.
C. Which files did the intruder browse and which were actually downloaded? Did the user understand how to navigate the system?
D. If access to the network came from the Internet, is it possible to identify nodes and IP addresses?
E. What has been the user's previous activity on this server and on the network prior to the incident?

Such inquiries establish a profile for the user before undertaking any interviewing. And, this preliminary information may be necessary for any computer forensic investigation. Defining a clear timetable for when system penetrations occurred forms a secure underpinning for the entire investigation.

Item three from the discovery points would require investigating who last signed out for the documents or computer media. (Hopefully, your company will have in place a documentation system to track custody of sensitive information. If it doesn't, the company may have more serious problems than just catching the thief.) In an interview with the custodial employee, determine if the materials were returned to safe storage. If they were returned, then have them explain the circumstances. Try to learn why the logging-in process failed. If the employee admits to not returning the materials, investigate fully the employee's explanation. Why were the materials left at that particular location? Did anyone else handle the documents or media? Was anyone else in the area? Has this oversight happened before? Why did it occur this time?

The purpose of this questioning is not to create a confrontation, but to acquire all the facts surrounding sensitive materials being in an unsecured place. An investigator should be firm, fair, and courteous and try to place the interviewee at ease. Even if the leaving out of sensitive materials, without a spy's malice, without any plotting to deprive the company of secrets, was an accident; unauthorized eyes passing by created an opportunity for compromise. Make the interviewee aware of the possible hazard. Focus, with your questioning, on identifying the universe of suspects.

Inadvertent references in an email (item four) or on an Internet site, speak quite loudly when discovered, far beyond what the message's writer intended. In emails, preserve the header information. It reveals the path an email took through cyberspace. The email software may not show the header directly with the body of the email. Sometimes, in the toolbar of the email program, the investigator will have to click on the feature "Reveal Code," "See Header," or something similar to make the header visible. Copy electronically any message postings on newsgroups or bulletin boards. Capture any email or Web addresses in the postings in an electronic file. Later investigation via a subpoena or a court order may reveal that a previously unknown email address actually belongs to someone inside or close to your company.

If the message or posting is on a site administered by an ISP (Internet Service Provider), then the ISP may cooperate with your investigation by at least identifying email addresses. However, do not be surprised if they require a court order before releasing any transaction details. Responsible ISP operators want to balance the privacy of their customers with the obligation to protect the public from crimes launched via cyberspace. If law enforcement is involved, ISP's generally want to avoid a search warrant being executed on their network, a potentially costly and disruptive event for them.

Item five involves a report by a co-worker, an informant, or a member of the security team. Based upon signs of suspicious activity (previously discussed in Chapter 8), the investigative response may require surveillance, a background investigation, and the association of the suspicious activity to a provable incident of industrial espionage. Building a timeline or a chronology may be necessary to demonstrate the association. Links to events in the company, in the marketplace, and in the suspects' lives all need documenting in the timeline model. (See Figure 10-2.)

Items six and seven share common ground. Social engineering preys upon people's desire to be helpful. Many times this approach works quite well, especially when a spy is smart enough to gather little bits and pieces of the puzzle from diverse sources within the target. The questioner doesn't ask for too much information from any one person, so the targets are less suspicious when questioned over the telephone or by email. Training employees about social engineering techniques will make them more aware of the dangers. As a part of that training, they should know where to report suspicious calls. When someone reports a social engineering attempt, try to obtain as much information about the caller as possible. Equally important, learning what information the caller was after can be essential to identifying what intellectual assets a potential spy seeks.

A description of the caller's voice, sex, relative age, the name used, any references given, and any callback number supplied, all of these details assist in a later investigation concerning those responsible. Interview other employees in the department to see if they received similar calls. Try to obtain the time of day when the calls came in. If possible develop a pattern to the attack on the company. Determine which individuals and departments the spy contacted. From the pattern, the investigation may identify a specific targeted project. If the targeted department does considerable interaction with other departments regarding the project, contact those other departments too.

If an employee feels "worked" or "pumped" for information at a technical meeting or conference, make sure they know how to report such an incident. When interviewing the employee, obtain a physical

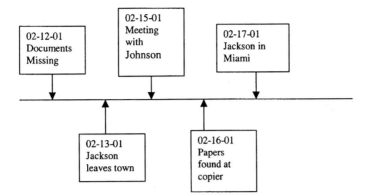

Figure 10-2. Timeline

description of the individual that questioned them. If group photos were a part of the meeting, get a copy of the one that contains the "suspect." Again, review with the employee the areas of technical interest by the acquaintance.

Talking to your employee is not necessarily illegal or even unethical, depending upon the approach used by the interviewer. The initial response to an incident like this one should be low-key. An incident report should go into the company's database, but avoid committing extensive investigative resources unless a red flag appears. The red flag will be if the same individual surfaces again, whether at another technical meeting or trade show, or by visiting your company under a cover or on a factory tour. Also, if the incident corresponds to another event, such as items 1-6 discussed above, you may be looking at the tip of an industrial espionage campaign against your business. As indicated in Chapters 8 and 9, correlating data makes or breaks discovering intelligence operations. Having in place an internal intelligence database and analytical software such as CaseRunner™ can help an investigator see the broad picture and develop connections between events that may remain unrelated otherwise.

The investigative steps in a proprietary theft inquiry include the following:

1. Recognition of a theft or the discovery of suspicious activity.
2. Incident report completed after initial interviews.
3. Comparison against the intelligence database. Preliminary analysis done.

4. If a correlation exists with other events, security creates an investigative plan with tentative suspects.

5. An impact analysis determines the possible extent of damage caused by a compromise. Immediate steps are taken to block any additional loss. If the impact is significant, a parallel investigation begins to establish the values for the trade secret(s) and the economic loss to the company. This investigation also develops evidence to prove the essential elements that the stolen material was a trade secret.

6. Fact gathering on the crime begins. This investigative path may employ interviews, surveillance, public record searches, securing evidence from the IT system and the Internet, and background investigations. Law enforcement may become involved at this stage. The company's investigation will coordinate with law enforcement. Obviously, in a major case the company's investigative role may be limited to locating internal records and resources.

7. The investigations are complete, and if the evidence warrants legal action, criminal prosecution or civil litigation, or possibly both proceedings begin.

8. Investigative support of the legal proceedings.

A WORD ABOUT CIVIL ACTIONS

Civil actions must conform to the general definition of what constitutes a "trade secret." If the owner of the trade secret has not taken reasonable steps to prevent its disclosure to the public, a civil case may not be successful. The owner would also have the burden of proof as to the secret's value. Unlike in a criminal case, the plaintiff would only have to show by the preponderance of the evidence that the defendant stole the trade secret. The "reasonable doubt" standard would not apply. It is quite conceivable that a criminal action could be decided in a defendant's favor, but the same defendant may lose a civil lawsuit. The "preponderance" standard, which requires simply presenting more credible evidence than the other side, is far less rigorous.

Since a defendant is not punished by incarceration, the goal in a civil case is to obtain damages in dollars against the defendant. A civil investigation must place equal energy into proving liability, that the defendant stole the trade secret, and that the theft warrants damages to compensate the plaintiff. If a jury does not believe your company's claim for damages, no matter the extent of the defendant's culpability, compensation may not be forthcoming. However, punitive damages may be an option in a case. Normally, juries award punitive damages for behavior that demonstrates "wanton, willful disregard for the rights of others." The applicability of punitive damages to trade secret theft depends upon the jurisdiction involved. In any event, proving damages whether compensatory or punitive is a critical part of a civil investigation.

Compensatory damages depend upon proving economic losses. What is important to remember is to be comprehensive in the proof but not outlandish. Inflating damages may turn the jury against your case. Remain reasonable.

Punitive damages depend upon the defendant's conduct. Carefully investigate all the details of the techniques used. If the evidence indicates particularly callous or amoral behavior by the defendant, it may have a role in establishing punitive damages.

BACKGROUND INVESTIGATIONS

When an employee comes under intense suspicion, then a background investigation should come into play. The aim of this investigation is to be as complete as possible without becoming unduly invasive. Preferably, the inquiry will be mainly public record searches. Those searches should include a check of the individual's driving history and any for any criminal record at the local and state level. If the driving record indicates accidents or convictions, then retrieve the relevant accident reports and court records. When a person has serious troubles in his or her life, they usually will run afoul of the law due to excessive drinking, drug use, or family conflicts. These criminal records are the first step in picking up on these problems. Make a part of your standard employment forms an authorization for the employee to sign, which allows the company to obtain driving records and to do a criminal background at any time during the individual's employment.

In addition, have a form for all new employees to sign that permits the company to conduct periodic background checks and to obtain credit histories on the employee at the company's expense. Obtaining a credit history will provide an overview of the subject's financial situation regarding debt. The history will key in on repossessions and foreclosures. It will also help to summarize the amount of debt and how well the subject pays on time. While the Fair Credit Reporting Act (FCRA) does allow accessing a credit history for employment purposes, I would not pull a suspected employee's credit report unless I already had a signed authorization in the employment file. Your company does not want to be in a gray area when it comes to the propriety of an investigation of an employee. Industrial espionage is a serious accusation to make against anyone, and they are not necessarily easy cases to prove. Therefore, do not give a suspect any possible ammunition against the company with allegations of FCRA violations.

The investigation should include a search for motor vehicles, boats, recreational vehicles, aircraft, and real estate in the subject's name. Again this information will provide a broader picture of the subject's financial condition. Since financial motives play a significant role in many industrial espionage cases, these records can be important in an investigation.

If license plate numbers, addresses, and telephone numbers become associated with the subject from public records or the credit history, then find out the owners or persons tied to those pieces of information. This additional research may uncover associates or accomplices. If the subject has an extensive residence history in another city, do a criminal background search at the local courthouse there too. At the Secretary of State's corporations office or division in your state capital, run an officer/director search under the subject's name. This search may uncover the subject's links to other companies. Also conduct at the same office a UCC (Uniform Commercial Code) filing search under the subject's name. This search may reveal loans or guarantees by a third party for a business owned by the subject or for improvements to the subject's home.

Finally, running the subject's name through the local newspaper's database and through LexisNexis may produce useful background data regarding arrests, accidents, and biographical facts. A search of civil records at the county and state levels is also in order. This search may reveal litigation involving the subject and useful background history.

The approach I recommend uses mainly public records. It may be better to collect documentary evidence at the start of a background investigation rather than rely on interviewing people who know the suspect. Asking questions can result in word getting back to the suspect. Answer as many questions you have about the suspect with records first, then you can expand the inquiry later to human sources if necessary. The things you do not want to do are going through the suspect's trash, conducting invasive surveillance, or sharing your suspicions about the individual with third parties (other than law enforcement). If you require the suspect's trash or residence examined, get law enforcement involved; they can obtain a search warrant if needed and if substantiated by the facts. Limited surveillance may be productive for a specific piece of information. For example, you might want to confirm the suspect meets an individual at a certain location. Don't park in the subject's neighborhood or in front of his girlfriend's house at night. If the case gets to that level, again involve law enforcement. Sharing your suspicions with outsiders about the suspect only invites a lawsuit.

DISCUSSION

1. How do the intelligence gathering process and investigation methods work hand-in-hand? (Does the intelligence system create collision points with industrial espionage that investigators can pick up on?)
2. In what ways can a computer forensics expert aid in an industrial espionage investigation?
3. Who should make the decision to bring in law enforcement in an *Economic Espionage Act* case? State your reasons for your answer.
4. Are prosecutions for trade secret theft in the best interest of a company? Argue both sides of the question.
5. Is stolen intellectual property difficult to trace? Explain your answer. State how you would uncover a paper or electronic trail from your company's repository into the hands of the spy and then into the client's hands.

CHAPTER NOTES

INTRODUCTION

The site for the American Society for the Advancement of Project Management is http://www.asapm.org/. Numerous other project management societies are available via an Internet search engine.

President Franklin Delano Roosevelt's "Four Freedoms" were a part of his January 6, 1941 State of the Union Address to Congress (Source: "Four Freedoms," *Academic American Encyclopedia,* Grolier, 1997).

For details about Vigenere ciphers, check out the Web site: http://www.trincoll.edu/depts/cpsc/cryptography/vigenere.html. And, Simon Singh's *The Code Book* (Doubleday, New York, 1999) has an interesting discussion about the Vigenère and other precomputer ciphers.

Just in case any skepticism exists about the daily, ongoing threat of industrial espionage, read "To Austin Startup Worker Was a Spy, Not a Moonlighter" by Cara Anna in the *Austin American-Statesman,* July 15, 2002. More about this case later, just note that industrial or corporate espionage can strike any business. In this incident, the alleged victim is a financial services company in Austin, Texas.

"The Future of Microcomputing," an article in the December 1996 issue of *Byte* magazine offers a glimpse at how computing systems are going to get smaller and more mobile. The URL for the article is http://www.byte.com/art/9612/sec6/art7.htm. *Pen Computing's* article, "Hawkins Keynote at Comdex 2001," provides a look at the past, present, and future of mobile computing. See http://www.pencomputing.com/palm/palmnews/palmnews-11-14-01.html.

For an example of "classic" physical security thinking, the reader should consider *Introduction to Security,* fifth edition by Robert J. Fischer and Gion Green, Butterworth-Heinemann, 1992. Part III, "Basics of Defense," summarizes the traditional American private security doctrine that evolved from Allan Pinkerton's time until the end of the Cold War.

CHAPTER 1

The information on the Chinese visiting the McDonnell Douglas plant in 1993 came from an account in John J. Fialka's *War by Other Means: Economic Espionage in America* (W.W. Norton, 1997). Fialka's "While America Sleeps," an article in the *Wilson Quarterly* (Winter 1997, Vol. 21, Issue1), and his *War by Other Means* provided Robert Cabot Lowell's history.

Lowell National Historical Park's Web site has an extensive bibliography on the development of Lowell, background on Robert Cabot Lowell, and a history of the textile industry in the city. The URL is http://www.nps.gov/lowe/loweweb/bibliography.htm.

For more information about Civil War ironclads check out the Web site: http://www.ameritech.net/users/maxdemon/ironintr.htm. The *Hunley* Web site is http://www.hunley.org/.

Several sources contributed to the American Civil War information surrounding Tredegar Iron Works and the attempts to build submarines and submersibles by the Confederacy. Charles B. Dew's *Ironmaker to the Confederacy, The War Between the Spies* by Alan Alexrod, *The Civil War* by Bruce Catton, *Fields of Battle* by John Keegan, and Harnett T. Kane's *Spies for the Blue and Gray,* all provided the necessary background. *The Pinkertons* by Richard Wilmer Rowan and *The Civil War Book of Lists* by Donald Cartmell yielded useful information. (See the Bibliography for full citations on the books.)

Also the Web sites, "U.S. Civil War Photographs, Tredegar Iron Works," authored by Robert F. Koch, at http://rkoch.internations .net/Civil_War/tredegar.html and "Tredegar Iron Works: The South's Major Arsenal" at http://civilwar.bluegrass.net/ArtilleryAndArms/tredegarironworks.html, provided helpful information on the layout and organization of Tredegar.

Check the works cited in the "For Further Reading" section at the end of the chapter to see the references used for the discussion of observation principles.

CHAPTER 2

My practical work experience with databases served as the basis for the SQL discussion. See Ronald L. Mendell's "Vulnerable Databases: Sleuthing with AWK and SQL," at http://www.info-sec.com/internet/01/internet_082101a_j.shtml.

Keeping Abreast of Science and Technology: Technical Intelligence for Business, Battelle Press, 1997, was the main source for the discussions of CTI and technical intelligence.

The Delphi poll has several variations, but basically it queries a panel of experts to obtain a consensus on an issue or to produce an "educated" prediction of the future. See "Predicting the Future: The Delphi Tradition" at http://www.personal.u-net.com/~acolyte/DelphicSpread.html.

John Michael Archer, *Sovereignty and Intelligence: Spying and Court Culture in the English Renaissance,* Stanford University Press, 1993 provides a good overview of the ideas of Francis Bacon regarding intelligence gathering. Oregon State University has *The New Atlantis* online at http://www.orst.edu/instruct/phl302/texts/bacon/atlantis.html.

Additional information about SQL is available from these Web sites: http://www.sqlcourse.com/ and http://www.w3schools.com/sql/ default.asp. The site "A Gentle Introduction to SQL" at http://sqlzoo.net/ is particularly instructive to beginners. For more background information on the SQL threat, read my article "Vulnerable Databases: Sleuthing with AWK and SQL" cited above.

CHAPTER 3

John Michael Archer's *Sovereignty and Intelligence: Spying and Court Culture in the English Renaissance* and Charles Nicholl's *The Reckoning* yielded the historical background on Christopher Marlowe and Elizabethan spying.

Winston Churchill's *A History of the English-Speaking Peoples: The Age of Revolution* and J.R. Harris' *Industrial Espionage and Technology Transfer: Britain and France in the 18th Century* contributed to the discussion of the eighteenth century. *Keeping Abreast of Science and Technology* was the source for Andrew Carnegie's quote. The reference to Robert Cabot Lowell is from John J. Fialka's *War by Other Means,* and his article "While America sleeps" discusses Michael Sekora. (See the Bibliography for complete citations.)

The London Crown Glass Company has a Web site on the history of plate glass making. This site's information contributed to the chapter's discussion. The URL for the site is http://www.londoncrownglass .co.uk/History.html.

CHAPTER 4

For the history of aerial spying investigate the National Air and Space Museum's Web, "The Spy Skies" at http://www.nasm.edu/galleries/lae/html/sky_early.htm.

Keeping Abreast of Science and Technology: Technical Intelligence for Business, Battelle Press, 1997 was the source for aerial ballooning during the American Civil War. John Keegan's *Fields of Battle* provided information about the Peninsular Campaign.

The information about R.V. Jones is from *The Wizard War* by R.V.Jones, 1978.

The Investigator's Little Black Book 2 by Robert Scott, (Crime Time Publishing, 1998) not only has references on aerial and satellite photography but also hundreds of other investigative sources.

Some of the insights on computer security came from *Countering Industrial Espionage,* authored by Peter A. Heims, 20th Century Security Education Ltd, 1982, and *Running a Ring of Spies* by Jefferson Mack, Paladin Press, 1996.

The title of *The Cuckoo's Egg* by Clifford Stoll, (Doubleday, 1989) derives from the fact that the cuckoo lays its eggs in other bird's nests, just like hackers and spies do on computer systems.

For technical explanations of "buffer overflows" and "smashing the stack" see *Hack proofing Your Network: Internet Tradecraft* edited by Ryan Russell and Stace Cunningham, Syngress, 2000.

The International PGP (Pretty Good Privacy) Home Page is http://www.pgpi.org/. A general site on cryptography is "Cryptography" (Copyright © Francis Litterio) at http://world.std.com/~franl/ crypto.html. Litterio recommends two newsgroups on cryptography: sci.crypt and sci.crypt.research. For an article about encryption for laptops, consider "Lost laptops compromise secrets," by Joshua Dean, October 1, 2001, at http://www.govexec.com/features/1001/1001managetech2.htm.

For references on laptop tracking software check out the following Web sites: http://www.stolenlaptop.com/, http://www.ztrace.com/, http://www. secure-it.com/laptrak/index.htm, http://www.pcguardian.com/, and http://www.stealthsignal.com/. This article, "Service finds stolen laptops" by Joel Smith, from: *The Detroit News* 10/24/00, provides an overview at http://www.usatoday.com/life/cyber/ccarch/ ccjoe038.htm.

Tips on preventing laptop computer theft are available at the University of Denver's Web site, http://www.du.edu/campus-safety/services/laptop. html and at the District of Columbia Metropolitan Police site at http://mpdc.dc.gov/info/consumer/laptop_theft.shtm. A discussion of branding laptops with a permanent label is at http://www. computersecurity.com/ stop/prevention.htm. A training film on laptop theft prevention is available for purchase through http://www.icontraining.com/ safeproduct/theft.htm.

An interesting article on wireless security is at "Beefing Up 802.11b Security: Standards group moving towards mending wireless security flaws," by Yardena Arar, PCWorld.com, Monday, February 04, 2002, http://www.pcworld.com/news/article/0,aid,82563,00.asp. Another article is at *PC Magazine* September 4, 2001, "Yes, wireless LANs are vulnerable, but yours doesn't have to be," by Craig Ellison; the URL is http://www.extreme-tech.com/article2/0,3973,11388,00.asp.

The list of mobile computing magazines is from http://newsdirectory.com/news/magazine/computer/mobile/.

The information about Standard Oil was from Titan: *The Life of John D. Rockefeller, Sr.* by Ron Chernow, Random House, 1998.

Trash raiding ideas derive from *Secrets of a Super Hacker* by the Knightmare, Loompanics Unlimited, 1994 and Ira Winkler's *Corporate Espionage*.

The account of Russian electronic eavesdropping came from an account in John J. Fialka's *War by Other Means*.

Building personal information from public records is discussed in *How to Do Financial Asset Investigations*, second edition by Ronald L. Mendell, Charles C Thomas, 2000.

The cloaking techniques discussed derive from my article, "Ask Me No Secrets, I'll Tell You No Lies" *(Security Management,* May 1994).

CHAPTER 5

"The development of private policing," by Susan Brenner, University of Dayton Law School, at http://cybercrimes.net/Private/early.html discusses Allan Pinkerton's early attempts at fighting industrial espionage.

On June 25, 1876 at the Philadelphia Centennial Exposition, Alexander Graham Bell demonstrated the telephone to Emperor Pedro II of Brazil. See the "Timeline of Alexander Graham Bell" at http://inventors.about.com/library/inventors/bltelephone6.htm.

Sherlock Holmes "commonplace books" contained indexes of information largely from the London newspapers about events and persons in Metropolitan London. Holmes referred to the books often in his investigations. He consulted the books in his famous case, "A Scandal in Bohemia," where he found a biography for his adversary, Irene Adler. The commonplace books resembled the paper-based newspaper morgue of the nineteenth and twentieth centuries prior to the electronic revolution. (Source: *The Encyclopedia Sherlockiana,* by Jack Tracy, Avenel Books, 1977.)

Databases like LexisNexis are ethically neutral. The information from them can be used for either good purposes or evil endeavors. It is in the best interest of our society to have as much public information available as possible, as long as it does not impinge upon traditionally private areas like medical information, family and sexual life, and financial information. We all just need to be aware that any publicly available information always may serve as a steppingstone to more private data. We do pay a price for living in an information-rich society with all of its advantages.

The EDGAR database complied by the Securities and Exchange Commission (SEC) can be found at http://www.sec.gov/edgar.shtml.

Database information about businesses from a competitive perspective is available from (1) "Competitive Intelligence Sources on the Internet" compiled by Joe Ryan at http://web.syr.edu/~jryan/infopro/intell.htm/, (2) Hoover's Online, http://www.hoovers.com, and (3) "Competitive Intelligence: A Librarian's Empirical Approach" at http://www.infotoday.com/searcher/sep00/gross.htm.

Robert Frost's "The Road Not Taken" is at http://www.robertfrost .org/.

See the notes for Chapter Nine below for Emerson's "Self-Reliance."

Henry David Thoreau's comments can be found in *Walden and Other Writings by Henry David Thoreau,* Bantam Books, 1989.

The ideas about attack trees arose from Bruce Schneier's *Secrets & Lies: Digital Security in a Networked World* (John Wiley & Sons, Inc., 2000). Attack trees are similar to fault trees used by engineers to isolate the causes for system failures.

Brainstorming ideas originated from Don Koberg and Jim Bagnall's *The Universal Traveler* (William Kaufman, 1976), Arthur B. Van Gundy's *108 Ways to Get a Bright Idea* (Prentice-Hall, 1983) and W. Gordon's *Synectics* (Harper & Row, out of print). Making the familiar strange is a central idea to Synectics, which uses metaphors and analogies to generate new ideas.

"Prosecuting Biotech Spy Cases Proves Nettlesome" by Paul Elias of the Associated Press appeared in the *Austin American-Statesman* in the August 5, 2002 edition. The news account deals with an alleged theft of stem cell materials from the University of California at Davis. Not only is the biotechnology industry under attack by industrial spies, but the article also points out that the *Economic Espionage Act of 1996* cases are hard to prosecute.

The Mole 2 aired on the ABC television network in late spring through midsummer 2002.

Sources for "Foreign Spies" and "Targets and Trends" included John J. Fialka's "While America Sleeps" and *War by Other Means,* "Global Intrigue on the Information Highway" *(Denver Post,* April 24, 1994), "Software Theft Suspect Under House Arrest" *(Seattle Times,* April 16, 1994), and Jean Guisnel's *Cyberwars: Espionage on the Internet* (Plenum Trade, 1997).

CHAPTER 6

The information about Standard Oil was from *Titan: The Life of John D. Rockefeller, Sr.* by Ron Chernow, Random House, 1998.

The case of alleged industrial espionage against Bristol-Myers regarding the manufacture of Taxol was from "For Pills, Not Projectiles," *Economist,* July 12, 1997.

Ideas about the "university research ploy" are based upon information in Fialka's article, "While America Sleeps."

Tesla and Marconi's patent dispute is from Marc J. Seifer's *Wizard, The Life and Times of Nikola Tesla,* Birch Lane Press, 1996 and in Margaret Cheney's *Tesla, Man Out of Time,* Dell Publishing, 1981.

Common ruses used by industrial spies are found in the article, "Defenses Against the Black Arts," by Alison Bass, *Darwin,* June, 2001.

Running a Ring of Spies by Jefferson Mack, Paladin Press, 1996, served as the source about false-flag recruitment and about sexy nightclubs in Vietnam doubling as intelligence collection agents for the Viet Cong. Observations about the Tet Offensive are from *Military Intelligence Blunders* by Col. John Hughes-Wilson, Carroll & Graf, New York, 1999.

An example of a power move against an individual company by an influential third party is in the article, "E-mail Shows Enron Official Urged Firm to Punish Broker Who Said 'Sell'," by Richard A. Oppel, Jr., *The New York Times,* in the *Austin American-Statesman,* March 27, 2002. The article alleges Enron Corporation pressured UBS Paine Webber to dismiss a broker for telling customers to sell the stock.

CHAPTER 7

The chapter is a "reverse" security survey from the perspective of the information thief. Intentionally, I am trying to shake up the perception that security is just a matter of instituting a list of countermeasures. The diversions listed by the spy are based upon real everyday experiences while doing security work at a telecommunications manufacturer over a period of months. I have encountered the burned coffee, employees' flat tires in the parking lot, doors jammed opened, and broken sprinkler heads. As far as we could discover, they were events not connected with a spy, but they managed to divert the resources of our force and vex our ability to protect assets. The spirit behind the spy's narrative is the books from the Rogue Warrior®, series by Richard Marcinko and John Weisman. (See as a starting point *Detachment Bravo,* Pocket Star Books, 2002.) While Marcinko speaks with a salty, coarse tongue, he has quite a bit of wisdom regarding circumventing security. Anyone interested in a different perspective should consider reading these books. For more information on conventional security surveys, consult James. F. Broder's *Risk Analysis and the Security Survey* (Butterworth-Heinemann, 1984, second edition 1999).

A freeware HEX editor, XVI32 is available at http://www.chmaas .handshake.de/delphi/freeware/xvi32/xvi32.htm. Another site for a free binary file editor called Frhed is at http://www.kibria.de/frhed .html.

I found numerous sites for obtaining office furniture keys on the Web. Of course, since these are all legitimate businesses offering a valuable service, I am not going to list them, because doing so could imply otherwise. It could also steer business that they do not desire their way. For a general article on how thieves defeat locks, please check out this Web site: http://www.mcevoy-lock.com/top-five-ways-thieves.htm. My source for information about boron-hardened steel shackles for padlocks was the hardware staff at the Home Depot. They advised that a boron-hardened shackle with an 11-mm diameter probably would be able to resist a small bolt cutter, but not a larger industrial-grade or a power-assisted cutter.

An excellent overview of the disposal issue for hard drives and other computer media is "End-of-Life Data Security in the Enterprise" by Anthony Thorton at http://www.redemtech.com/extaudit//news_research/ds_whitepaper.pdf.

A guide to the basics of computer forensics is available at "Computer Forensics & Evidence," http://www.computer-data-forensics-evidence-discovery.com/.

For an overview on information security for generalists in the profession, please consult my article, "Home Sweet Home? Protection Sensitive Information: A Primer for Executives" at the Web site: http://www.gwsae.org/ExecutiveUpdate/2000/September/HomeSweet .htm.

The book by Bryan Pfaffenberger, *Protect Your Privacy on the Internet,* (John Wiley & Sons, Inc., 1997), has an informative chapter on what constitutes strong passwords and how to generate them.

CHAPTER 8

The quote from *The Prince* by Niccolo Machiavelli is in the Bantam Classics edition of 1966, translated by Daniel Donno.

For a site on privacy violations by an employer go to http:www. divorcelawinfo2.com/mylawyer/. Go to the "Law Guide" section and look under the category, "Employer's Rights." It has a discussion on privacy issues.

An alternate way to access the information is to go to http://www. mylawyer.com. Again, this information is for background only and should not substitute for actual legal counsel.

CaseRunner is described in detail at http://www.caserunner.com/.

A good source for information about how an IT expert would trace intrusions into a network is the book, *Hacker's Challenge,* edited by Mike Schiffman, (McGraw-Hill, 2001). It is fairly technical, but it does demonstrate how an intrusion investigation builds from the various monitoring logs available.

CHAPTER 9

"Warez" sites are clearinghouses for pirated software. Run the term on any Internet search engine like Google and see what you get.

The Society of Competitive Intelligence Professionals at http://www. scip.org has a large number of books, publications, and audio tapes on various techniques and methods for business and competitive intelligence that the security professional may find as useful background.

Emerson's "Self-Reliance" may be found in *Selected Essays, Lectures, and Poems of Ralph Waldo Emerson,* edited by R.E. Spiller (Pocket Books, 1965).

Observations on the obsolescence of security equipment are based upon personal work experiences in security at two high-tech companies. A good resource to monitor changes in security technology is *Security Management* magazine. Their Web site is http://www.securitymanagement.com.

Some of the ideas about external intelligence are based upon the book, *How to Conduct Business Investigations and Competitive Intelligence Gathering* by Ronald L. Mendell (Thomas Investigative Publications, Austin, Texas, 1997).

CHAPTER 10

To see an actual colonial indenture agreement, visit the Web page, http://members.aol.com/ntgen/hrtg/indenture.html.

Punitive damages are permitted in cases involving the theft of trade secrets. See the Web site, "Trade Secret Law: Overview" by Stephen Elias, Nolo Press 1998 at http://www.markeyingtoday.com/legal/ tradesec.htm.

For two fairly contemporary cases involving alleged trade secret theft, please refer to "To Austin Startup Worker Was a Spy, Not a Moonlighter" in the *Austin American-Statesman* by Cara Anna, July 15, 2002 and "The Con's Latest Ploy" (X-IT vs. Kidde) in *White-Collar Crime Fighter,* Vol. 4, No. 3,

March 2002 (http://www.wccfighter.com). The first case demonstrates that the defense in a trade secret case will always argue, and rightly so, given this is a gray area, that the "trade secret" was in fact not a trade secret. In the second case, Kidde, a ladder manufacturer, was found by a jury in Virginia to have used patent information from another company illegally and to have violated a confidentiality agreement. (The case, of course, is still subject to appeal by Kidde.) Always obtain confidentiality agreements when working with outsiders. Obtain similar agreements with your employees.

For a good nutshell review of computer forensics, the Web site, "Computer Forensics & Evidence" at http://www.computer-data-forensics-evidence-discovery.com/index.htm is an excellent summary that shows deleting information from a hard drive involves more than just clicking on the mouse or tapping a few keys.

The Economic Espionage Act of 1996 is at http://execpc.com/~mhallign/federal.html.

The Fair Credit Reporting Act is at http://www.ftc.gov/os/statutes/fcra.htm.

CHRONOLOGY

The information about Timothy Webster is from the William Gilmore Beymer Papers, "Timothy Webster: Spy," at The Center for American History, The University of Texas at Austin and from *The Pinkertons: A Detective Dynasty* by Richard Wilmer Rowan (Little, Brown, and Company, 1931).

Keeping Abreast of Science and Technology: Technical Intelligence for Business, Battelle Press, 1997 was the source for aerial ballooning during the American Civil War.

Information about the Norden bombsight and Russian knowledge of the Atomic bomb are from Richard S. Friedman's review, "War by Other Means," from *Parameters: U.S. Army War College,* Autumn, 1998.

"Industrial Espionage" by Edward E. Furash was in the December 1959 *Harvard Business Review.*

"The Open Barn Door: U.S. Firms Face a Wave Of Foreign Espionage" by Douglas Waller appeared in *Newsweek,* May 4, 1992.

MASTER CHECKLIST

Spies' Shopping List:

1. Identifying parts and materials used in manufacture. (Also identifying sources.)
2. Understanding industrial processes and manufacturing steps.
3. The amounts of raw materials and finished goods on hand.
4. Proprietary techniques, formulas, and control systems used.
5. Software and computer systems employed.
6. Production schedules, shifts, and the number of workers employed. The number of workers in each job classification.
7. Production records, reports, lab notes, or engineering reports and drawings.
8. Machinery or equipment used.
9. Physical dimensions and layout of the plant.
10. Physical characteristics of support areas such as incoming roads, rail-roads, waterways, docks, parking lots, and employee facilities such as the cafeteria and break areas.
11. Financial records pertaining to manufacture.
12. Marketing records or sales records pertaining to production or manu-facture.
13. Any production problems at the site.
14. Any construction in progress at the site.
15. Security measures in place at the facility.

If the target contains a research facility, then the intelligence effort will seek:

A. Relevant contents of research databases.
B. The identity and job descriptions of key research staff.
C. Project plans, descriptions, and progress reports.
D. Research supplies, materials, and equipment used.
E. Project managers' reports.
F. Costs or cost accounting records associated with projects.
G. Any prototypes, models, or preproduction goods.

The shopping list for the technological spy also would include:

A. Identifying emerging technologies that the target has within its organization. (Just because the target possesses a nifty technology doesn't mean they will exploit its potential. Xerox gave Apple the idea for the graphical interface that became Apple's operating system. Xerox failed to exploit the potential.)

B. Recognizing shifts in technology and their impact on the target. Is the target working on research projects likely to succeed or will they be dead ends? (Delphi polling may help in this analysis.)

C. Comparing substitute or competing technologies and predict the target's response to them. (Will the target stay on its own path or will it adopt other points of view in developing a new technology?)

D. Recognizing marketing influences on the target's research programs.

Checklist for an Office Walk-Through:

1. What is visible on blackboards, whiteboards, and calendars?
2. Documents found around the copying machine and the nearby trash basket.
3. Can you gain access to labs and testing areas? How about the computer operations center?
4. In production areas, are equipment, materials, and workstations labeled in a way that gives clues to outsiders as to what is going on? Can they build the steps in the production (manufacturing) process from the signage?
5. Visit the outside trash bin or dumpster. Are intact, legible documents in the trash? How about computer media? If you run the computer media such as floppy disks on a machine, what can you see?

Researcher's Communications:

How a researcher communicates information about his or her research. The following information paths are available to a researcher:

1. Lab notebooks.
2. Entries to internal research databases.
3. Internal email with other workers.
4. Memorandums and reports to company management. Possibly some internal company publications.
5. Open source company publications such as the annual report.
6. Open source trade, technical, or scientific magazines and journals.
7. Speeches or presentations to professional societies. Testimony before governmental bodies.
8. External email with other colleagues in the field.

9. Postings on Web sites, newsgroups, or electronic bulletin boards.
10. Profiles or interviews for the science or technical press. Or, general science articles written by the researcher.

Knowledge-Based Attacks:

A knowledge-based attack will look to the following:

1. Identify research relevant to the client's needs. And, who at the target is doing that research. (The spy who has done her homework knows where to go shopping.)
2. Determine which research communities are the most productive. (The spy can concentrate on places that offer the greatest yield.)
3. Identify who the key players are within the target. (This sifting out process narrows the field of employees that require background research and monitoring.)
4. Form a strategy for intelligence gathering against the target. (A penetration plan may not be necessary if all the required intelligence can be gathered from open sources. Or, preliminary intelligence efforts will reduce the need for internal operations within the target and minimize the risk of detection or exposure.)
5. Gather clues or partial information as to the contents of items 1-4. (Uncovering one fact makes it easier to discover other information. It is like finding steppingstones across a pond or a creek. Once one learns the geography, navigating a path to the desired information becomes easier.)

Sources for Knowledge-Based Attacks:

- Commercial databases like Dialog® and LexisNexis™.
- Patent literature.
- Trade and industry journals.
- Dialog's NewsRoom.
- *Scientific American* and *Science* magazines.
- Abstracts of technical meetings.
- Science databases.
- Testimony before state and federal regulatory agencies.
- Reports on the results of research grants.
- Company annual reports.
- SEC filings.
- Trend studies by industry analysts.
- Investment analysts' reports.
- Directories and biographical encyclopedias.
- Classified ads for scientific or research positions.

Aerial Observation:

Aerial observation focuses on the following indicators, which tell a fairly complete story of what is going on at a plant:

1. *Use.* Wear on roads, railroad tracks, loading docks, and on parking areas. Ruts in dirt roads or on the shoulders of paved roads, skid or tire marks on pavement, excessive potholes on paved surfaces, shiny railroad tracks, and goods piled on docks are all signs of heavy use.
2. *Numbers.* Employees outside at lunch hours or at change of shift, delivery trucks, roads and rail lines serving the site, water towers or water reservoirs for fire protection or industrial processing, electrical lines and substations, buildings and support structures, above ground pipe and conduits,
3. *Amounts.* Equipment, raw materials, trash bins, emissions. Taking photographs at different times of the day over a period of a couple of weeks will provide enough information to make estimates of the production flow through the site.
4. *Changes.* Buildings under construction or being torn down; relocations of equipment, materials and goods; roads, waterways, or railroad spurs under construction; additional power resources.

The Points of Computer Vulnerability to Watch Are:

A. Technology or Process
   1. *Interception of communications:* terminal, telephone line, or telephone junction box.
   2. *At the monitor:* photographing or printing the screen, piggybacking (using someone else's monitor or terminal while they are away but are still logged in), and unauthorized access (using another's password and login).
   3. *Disk Drives:* diskettes copied or stolen and files erased (sabotage).
   4. *Magnetic Tape Drives:* copied or stolen or tapes erased; substituted with erroneous data on the tape (another form of sabotage).
   5. *Printers:* extra unauthorized copies of reports and documents printed. Confidential documents seen by unauthorized eyes at printer, and documents photocopied or photographed.
   6. *Waste:* paper captured from the trash, computer media retrieved and read, and "obsolete" computers having their hard drives read.
B. People
   1. *Clerical:* steal data, alter or forge data.
   2. *Computer Operators and Users:* copy files, sabotaging of data.
   3. *Programmers:* theft of proprietary software or data, unauthorized altering of programming code.

What will a spy look for when penetrating your IT security? A spy's checklist would include:

1. Personal information about high-level users. This data may lead to cracking passwords since users tend to create passwords derived from their daily lives. (See Chapter 5 for a detailed discussion.)
2. Access rights to computers or servers used by key personnel.
3. Raid the trash for computer printouts and tossed media like floppies.
4. Find hiding places in user's desks for passwords, floppies containing sensitive data, and notebooks (of the paper kind) containing logins and passwords.
5. Gain computer information via indirect methods. Can computer screens be seen from the street using high-powered binoculars? Or, can the spy pick up electronic emanations or computer wireless transmissions from a nearby observation post?

As a security specialist, possible countermeasures you could implement include:

1. Place password generation controls into your security program. They can prevent short passwords based upon personal information.
2. Enforce lockup procedures for computer media containing sensitive files when not in use. Train employees in how to reduce computer notebook theft. Make employees aware that a vendor, a housekeeper, a janitor, or a new acquaintance could be a spy. Point out that leaving sensitive material out and unattended only makes life easy for information thieves.
3. Make sure employees know how to use correctly any encryption software provided.
4. Tell employees that what they consider to be good hiding places rarely work. Inquisitive minds do find sticky notes under the desktop or in the book in the corner. If keeping track of multiple passwords becomes too tiresome, then suggest placing them in an encrypted electronic file. The file's pass phrase will be long enough to make it hard to crack. Preferably, the phrase should be something easy to remember, but difficult to guess. "Spies do not wear purple eyeglasses" is arbitrary, and a bit silly, but it is easy to remember and long enough to resist brute force attacks.
5. Install appropriate window shades or screens to prevent viewing monitors from the street. Have an electronics countermeasures expert measure the size of the emanations shadow cast by your terminals and monitors or by computer wireless operations. Install any shielding recommended by your expert.

Assuming total computer security at any facility invites folly. Computer security will always fall short for the following reasons:

1. A large percentage of passwords and logins are not that hard to guess or to crack. To maintain a high level of password security requires a Herculean effort with constant friction against human nature.
2. Workers leave their systems logged in while they go on break or to lunch or even when they leave for the night. Piggybacking becomes a tactic fairly easy to employ.
3. People with high-level access can be compromised by bribery or by threat of reprisal.
4. Once data stops being electrons and takes physical form on paper, microfiche, unencrypted files on disks, or stored on tape, it becomes much easier to steal.

Some IT countermeasures do cause a spy problems. Keep an eye out for the following:

A. Good password controls. (Passwords are long, unpredictable in content, which means a high level of randomness, and get changed regularly.)
B. Audit controls are in place. All network activity gets logged. (To check and see the extent of this activity, piggyback on someone else's login and try to access a file they don't have privileges for. Check later to see if they get a security email about it. A one-time attempt shouldn't cause much of a stir; it will be dismissed most likely as an error.)
C. The network has good segmenting using firewalls, proxy servers, and routers. (If you go into your MS.DOS window, you can't change the drive directory to drives and servers outside of your segment.)
D. Effective encryption is in place. (Files and databases are encrypted using publicly tested encryption algorithms like Triple-DES, and PGP. Look for policies regarding encryption on the company's Intranet site. Emails transmitting public-keys, the use of PGP in emails, and employee training classes on encryption procedures are all signs of heavy encryption use.)
E. Network intrusion detection is in place. (Do a buffer overflow attack on the target's network login software. Try to go on the system a few days later using the same attack. If you can't do a login, it is a good sign intrusion detection is going on and logs are being checked regularly.)

Electronic Eavesdropping:

The steps toward electromagnetic security should include:

- Assess your client's real vulnerabilities. If a spy does intercept your telecommunications, wireless cellular and network traffic, or digital emanations, what is the worst that will happen?
- Consider how much your client is "in play" as far as potential industrial espionage goes. Do your client's products and services offer a prime target? Is your client in an industry that has large-scale industrial espionage activity? (This evaluation will require external intelligence gathering, which we discussed in Chapter 9)
- If the risks are unacceptable, which means intercepts could cause grave harm, then institute a countermeasures program. Start with the basics: encrypt computer traffic wherever feasible and perform good physical security on in-house telecommunications facilities. Make sure all telephone and utility closets are locked down when not in use. And, when vendors enter these areas, insure that they have an escort. Have security patrols regularly check these areas to make sure they remained locked. The same procedures apply to server and network hub rooms.
- If you suspect someone is planting bugs or is doing a digital emanation capture, call in professional help. Common places for bugs include inside telephones, inside wall outlets, or under desks. Favorite places for taps include telecommunications closets, network hub rooms, and utility closets. Signs of digital emanation capture include suspicious vans parked near your facility or monitoring equipment found on your property. When in doubt, bring in some qualified assistance.
- An electronic countermeasures professional should have extensive background and training from the military or law enforcement in this area. Plus, he or she should possess a Bachelor of Science or an M.S. degree in electronic or electrical engineering. Always obtain references from the expert on other corporate clients.

Extramural Users of Sensitive Files:

1. *Vendors.* Consider the people who actually work with the data like in the Tech Advocates case and the transporters of the information such courier services.
2. *Suppliers.* These companies may need access to sensitive specifications in order to deliver the necessary components or raw materials.
3. *Consultants.* The persons may have to take sensitive information with them to do research.
4. *Government and Regulatory Agencies.* They may handle sensitive information to process permits, licenses, product applications, and so on.
5. *Telecommuting Employees.* Not only do they take home sensitive documents and files, but also the remote accessing of sensitive electronic data is becoming the norm for this group. Many companies use a VPN

(Virtual Private Network) to allow the safe transmission of data over the Internet, but are these workers keeping their end of the connection secure? Most people feel secure in their homes, so leaving computers logged in but unattended is a real danger. Also, password security remains a real question. Are passwords scribbled on the desk pad? Is the corporate password the same one the employee uses for accessing personal ISP providers such as Prodigy, AOL, and the like?

6. *Traveling Employees.* These persons face similar dangers to those of the telecommuters. They also face a greater risk of computer laptop theft. And, while hotel rooms may afford psychological security, in reality many people have access to your room in a hotel. So, these workers need to be careful regarding what they leave in their rooms, especially in the trash.

Prime Targets for Foreign Espionage:

What key industries will spies be targeting? The prime targets are:

Aerospace
Biotechnology
Software
Automobile Manufacturing
Pharmaceutical Manufacturing

Dealing with Disinformation Attacks:

Industries particularly vulnerable to this discrediting tactic are:

1. Those companies engaged in genetic research. (Wild stories of mutant viruses and bacteria incite public hysteria.)
2. Nuclear industries. (Allegations of faulty safety measures or of contamination.)
3. Pharmaceutical firms. (Safety problems with drugs or allegations of contamination.)
4. Food producers and distributors. (Allegations of contamination.)
5. Computer manufacturers. (Faulty hardware or microchips.)
6. Software manufacturers. (Bug-ridden software, software failures.)

Of course, we are talking about false allegations suddenly appearing on the Internet. Inquiries by legitimate organizations like governmental agencies, responsible consumer groups, and responsible journalists are a totally different matter. Disinformation campaigns require a response developed and planned well in advance of any crisis. This ultimate power play by an adversary demands a reasoned, professional response, which is difficult to do under pressure. The chances for coping with an emergency like this improve with good preparation. Those preparations should cover the following areas:

1. Have forensic services in place to determine the actual origin point of emails and Web postings.
2. Establish a crisis management team to contact customers, vendors, regulatory agencies, suppliers, and the media with the correct facts.
3. Create the ability to deploy rapidly a rumor hotline to handle inquiries by customers, the press, stockholders, business partners, and employees.
4. Establish an investigative team to separate fact from fiction regarding the allegations.
5. Insure that the media or public relations unit has the capability to issue timely announcements on the Internet and to the press during a crisis.

Good Document Controls:

Good document controls will include:

A. Dual control of trade secrets. One person alone should not be able handle and remove the documents.
B. Tight sign-in and sign-out procedures. Both authorized persons must be present to complete these steps.
C. A secure work area for highly sensitive documents and trade secrets. It should be physically and electronically isolated from the rest of the facility.
D. Twenty-four security or monitoring of the storage area for these secrets. (Usually via an alarm system and video surveillance.)
E. Finally, electronic transfers of trade secrets need protection with strong encryption and by transfer through a secure channel like a VPN (Virtual Private Network).

Whenever dealing with other businesses where discussions involving trade secret information may be necessary, always obtain nondisclosure and confidentiality agreements.

Security Guidelines for University and Independent Facilities:

Be careful to insure that research programs conducted outside of your portals follow these guidelines:

1. Physical and electronic separation of different projects. This safeguard includes both records and research personnel.
2. Proper storage facilities for proprietary data and documents. Locking up data is essential.

3. Adequate access controls to computer databases. The use of passwords and encryption as needed.

4. Access controls to research labs and work areas. One project's badges and access cards should not allow entry to another project's areas.

5. Security audits done jointly by the university or the independent lab during the life of the contract.

6. The right of final approval on any persons granted access to restricted areas or information.

7. Exercise the right to have unannounced security inspections.

Observational Program for Security Patrols:

As far as observational practices go, here are my suggestions:

1. When officers conduct a patrol, have them complete a checklist form showing where, when, and what they checked. If there are particularly sensitive areas from an information security standpoint that require regular inspection, please include them on the form. Remember your officer's shadow appearing about the premises is a spy's nemesis.

2. Have different patrol routes established, which will be used in the course of a shift. One route may take in safety inspection points such as sprinkler system pressure, alarm panel status, refrigerator temperatures, heating and air conditioning systems status, and boiler system pressures. Another patrol may go by all key computer systems areas like the operations center, server rooms, computer labs, printer areas, telecommunications rooms and closets, and media storage areas. Other patrols will include checking copying, faxing, and document preparation areas and doing inspections for contraband. Just make sure any shift has a mix of the different patrols.

3. Specific things to look for on a patrol include:
   a. Inspect exterior doors and locks.
   b. Check all padlocks to critical areas. Verify the serial number of the locks and that the security officer's key works the lock.
   c. Check all internal doors to critical areas such as labs, computer rooms, document and computer media storage rooms, and executive offices.
   d. Test the functioning of any access controls such as card readers to internal areas.
   e. Walk through all areas where access to sensitive information is possible, whether that access is by computer terminal or by paper documents. If workers are present beyond their normal shift, politely check identification.

f. Look for computer monitors or terminals left on and logged in, but the user is not present. Document any such incidents with a report and secure the machine.

g. Check file cabinets containing sensitive documents that have left unlocked and unattended. Again document the incident and secure the cabinets. (Develop a color-coded labeling scheme for such cabinets so that they can be spotted easily by security.)

h. Locate any notebook, laptop, or palm-sized computers left unattended. Document and secure the items. Leave a notice telling the user what has been removed and where he or she can claim it.

i. Check all fax, copy machine areas, and shredder bin areas for sensitive documents or materials. If the machines have locking capabilities, insure that they are locked or that the activation module or counter has been removed. Fax machines may need to be on 24 hours a day. If so, make sure the security officers know where to secure any nighttime faxes for retrieval by first shift. And, very important, security patrols should understand how to do a purge printout listing of the last ten to 20 faxes. (If security finds sensitive documents at any of the above locations, have a procedure in place to secure them and to document the event.)

j. For any company, I recommend having a "clean desk" policy for when employees leave for the day. If your company doesn't have one, then it is only doing me a favor. Make sure security documents any violations of a clean desk policy and that they secure any sensitive materials. (There may be projects that require numerous documents being left out. If so, place those projects in a special room that is locked at the end of each workday.)

k. Check behind the vending machines, in the refrigerators, above the ceiling tiles in the employee locker room, in the first aid kits, in the janitorial closets, and in the supply storage areas for contraband. Always keep your security force in the habit of looking in the crannies and crevices. It will keep them in form as good observers. And, it helps cast a broad security shadow on the plant.

l. Check loading docks and hallways for documents or computer media left there in error. (Again, have procedures to document the event and to remove the materials to a secure area.)

m. Have special projects for security patrols. One evening they may inspect, for example, all utility and telecommunications closets for signs of tampering, bugging, or break-in.

Most important, security managers should check on security officers to see that they conduct effective patrols. Planting test documents and simulated contraband periodically will keep them on their toes.

Watching for Suspicious Activity:

Security can start coming after industrial spies by keeping track of the following:

1. People working unusual hours alone.
2. Employees found in areas not normally associated with their job.
3. Vendors found in areas not necessary for their work or in unauthorized areas.
4. Unusual events such as the diversion tactics in Chapter 7
5. Employees sharing suspicions with security personnel.
6. Copy machines being used at unusual hours.
7. People who are not employees hanging around in the parking lot or who appear to be checking out the perimeter of the building.
8. People going through the trash or through items left on the loading dock.
9. Persons trying to gain access to critical areas without valid access cards.
10. Employees without badges or proper identification in the facility.
11. Employees with guests who have not been signed in and who do not possess visitors' badges.
12. Employees trying to remove computers, equipment, or sensitive records without the required property passes or documentation.
13. Employees or vendors bringing in outside computers, cameras, or computer media without appropriate written permission.
14. Any indication of computer "piggybacking." Someone using another user's terminal without doing his or her own login procedure.
15. Any indication of trying to by-pass physical security measures. These events range from rigging a door to stay open to disabling an access control device to turning off a video surveillance camera.

When these events occur, security officers should create a report that answers the five fundamental questions: Who, Where, When, Why, and How? The question, "Who is involved?" is the most critical.

Creating a Security Policy:

Ideally, the creation of a policy would contain the following steps:

1. Identify critical information assets that require constant protection. (This step is not a one-time action. It requires periodic reevaluation. And, management has the obligation to notify the security manager

when the assets or their rankings change. Protecting everything with high-level resources is not feasible. So, management has to choose which assets will receive the greatest protection.)

2. Create rings of protection around those assets. These rings may involve a mix of Information Technology (IT) security, physical security, and alarm systems. Overlapping design becomes a critical factor. If one element fails, then another should be able to step in and protect the asset. So far, this approach constitutes traditional security doctrine. But, as indicated earlier in the text, static perimeter security, while not obsolete, faces shortcomings in a world of increasingly mobile information. Therefore, any defense plan also must accommodate the guarding of sensitive data when it passes outside of the traditional perimeter.

3. Devise smooth handoffs between different security elements. For example, IT personnel may have rock-solid network security procedures in place. However, once a user prints documents containing sensitive data, those documents need protection throughout their lifecycle or until the value of the information expires. The IT staff needs to work with users to insure they transfer documents needing storage or destruction directly to the security staff or to a bonded service hired for those purposes. In the converse, if security normally posts an officer at the computer operations center's entrance, then an emergency transfer of that officer requires a backup plan to come into play. Someone from the IT staff needs to fill in at that post until the officer can return.

4. Security personnel, IT personnel, and users of sensitive information all need to understand their role in information security. Basic counterespionage training for these individuals should include:

   a. Defining industrial or corporate espionage.

   b. Identifying the methods of attack commonly used:

      1. Diversion of security forces.

      2. Social engineering.

      3 Recruitment of employees.

      4. Penetration techniques such as piggybacking and working under a cover.

   c. Explaining the lifecycle of sensitive, proprietary information. Defining the difference between confidential information and trade secrets. (Confidential information contains data that is in the company's best interests not to be made public. Or, it may be information that the company has a legal obligation to keep secure, such as employee medical records for example. Trade secrets constitute an actual intellectual asset of the business. See Chapter 10 for a complete discussion.) Why must these sensitive records and information remain secure at their creation, during their use, in storage, and at their destruction. How users, IT personnel, and the security force all have a role to play in protection.

d. Giving suggestions to improve:
  1. Developing communications between different departments. (Who to call when something happens.)
  2. The handling and care of sensitive documents. (When to lock them up will been upon the operational needs of the business.)
  3. The classifying of sensitive documents. (The categories of sensitive documents or files again will depend upon the nature of the company's business. Classification procedures will include color coding, using security headers and footers on documents, the stamping of documents with security labels, marking bulk documents, especially those for destruction, and whose responsibility is it to classify and mark sensitive documents.
  4. Identifying critical areas such as labs, computer operation centers, telecommunications rooms, mailrooms, printer and fax areas, and copy machine rooms. And discussing the vulnerabilities associated with those areas.
  5. Discussing how to report suspicious events or activities.

Build into the protection system intelligence gathering operatives. Develop human assets to provide internal intelligence feedback. These operatives will come from among your security force and from regular workers willing to be eyes and ears. These individuals will receive advanced intelligence training.

The Industrial Espionage Process:

Industrial espionage is a process. An informant needs to understand the steps in that process. Those steps are:

1. *Initial Research.* Learning about the target from open sources to determine the best way to conduct the espionage campaign. (At this point in the cycle, an informant may observe an employee or a vendor trying learn about areas in the company outside of their area of normal responsibility.)
2. *Penetration or Recruitment.* The spy penetrates the target or finds someone internal to acquire the information. (Signs of penetration range from evidence of a break-in to discovering people in unauthorized areas. Signs of recruitment may include sudden reversals of fortune in finances or in the employee's social life.)
3. *Compromising Sensitive Information.* The actual theft of information occurs. (The telltale signs include the hacking of and penetrations of IT systems, the temporary removal of documents, the outright theft of documents, and the less than clandestine copying of sensitive docu-

ments. Spies or compromised employees sometimes get sloppy and leave documents out. Or, the security force can interrupt them, and then they do not get everything put away in time.)

4. *Endgame.* The spy turns over the product to his or her client. The espionage operation normally comes to an end. (Again the spy or her associates can get careless here. They may not terminate the mission smoothly by neglecting to erase all the paper and electronic trails behind them. The goal of the internal intelligence program to prevent them from coming in and out cleanly. Hopefully, parts of the counter-intelligence effort will stick to them, providing clues for later investigation.)

5. *Disclosure.* The sensitive proprietary data finally enters the marketplace. Or, confidential data becomes public. This may be the first time that the target realizes that industrial espionage has occurred.

An informant's training needs to point out that most likely they will catch an industrial espionage case well past the first step.

How the Security Manager Monitors the Company's Business:

A security manager will acquire knowledge about the company from:

A. The Annual Report
B. Internal Company Publications
C. News Accounts
D. Industry Journals and Trade Magazines
E. Industry Analyst Reports on the Company
F. Comparisons Made in the Press with Competitors
G. Attendance at Business Conferences and Meeting
H. Attendance at Company Meetings

This information provides the necessary background to judge how events in the business arena will impact the company's operations.

The BI Unit's Sources:

Main sources of information to the BI unit include:

1. Access to major databases such as Dialog, Profound, and LexisNexis.
2. Major Industry Trade Journals and magazines.
3. S/P/E sources such as *The New York Times, The Washington Post, The Los Angeles Times, Business Week,* and *The Economist.*
4. Field intelligence reports from the sales force, marketing, and the technical staff.
5. Interviews with key persons in the industry.
6. Analyst's reports.

At first look the work of the BI unit may seem slightly alien to what security does. Instead, view the BI unit as a direct supplement to security's own knowledge base.

Economic Espionage Unit:

Typical external sources for the EEU would include the following:

1. Scanning for information on the Internet about the company. This data comes from a wide range of sites: hacker sites, newsgroups, business sites, political activist pages, warez pirated software sites, and those Web locations that are industry related. Gaining a broad view of what is being said about the company online is the goal. This focused surfing technique also picks up actionable intelligence. A hacker may be passing on a tip about a flaw that they've found in the company's security defenses.
2. Reviewing competitor actions and developments. (Supplied by BI unit.)
3. Networking with other security professionals in the private and public sectors. This interaction identifies emerging information security threats.
4. Monitoring the major publications in the security field for emerging threats and trends. Also, the unit studies incidents involving industrial espionage.
5. Checking the general press for cases involving industrial espionage. As a supplement to this review, the unit runs inquiries on say LexisNexis based upon probable threats. For example, "Industrial Espionage-Plant Genetics" produces cases, stories, or incidents relevant to that area of biotechnology. Such research may provide sufficient details to assist in investigating a case or to prevent a similar incident from occurring. Again, this database can be a shared resource between the EEU and the BI units.
6. Following industrial espionage investigations when the trail of evidence leads outside of the company's walls. Such an outreach may involve background investigations of suspects and coordination with law enforcement.
7. Interrogating the company's security incident database looking for connections between external events and internal incidents. (Both internal incidents and external events, which could have a security impact, go into the incident database.) An internal pattern of industrial espionage may not become apparent unless correlated against external events. Detecting subtle patterns often requires first knowing what to look for.

Knowledge of criminal activity elsewhere enables the latent to become visible in your backyard. (See Table 9-4.)

The security manager should regularly receive the BI unit's intelligence product like other leaders in the company. This information should be correlated with the product from the EEU. Ideally, the BI and EEU units will share information base upon common interests.

Investigative Checklist for Trade Secrets Theft.

These are the key points in an I.E. investigation. (See also Figure 10-1.)

1. Identify evidence that a theft or conversion by deception or fraud has occurred. Evidence of unauthorized access would also be acceptable.
2. Establish that the object of the crime was a trade secret.
3. Develop evidence of a foreign government's involvement in the theft.
4. In the alternative, establish evidence of a product in interstate or foreign commerce.
5. Identify the parties responsible for the crime.
6. Do background investigations on the suspects.
7. Establish the value of the trade secret. And, establish the value of the loss caused by the trade secret's theft.
8. The investigations are complete, and if the evidence warrants legal action, criminal prosecution or civil litigation, or both, proceedings begin.
9. Investigative support of the legal proceedings.

Discovering Industrial Espionage:

Discovery points include:

1. Other companies place into the marketplace products based upon your trade secret.
2. An audit trail on the IT system reveals unauthorized access to sensitive files.
3. Sensitive documents or media are found left outside of secure storage or in an unauthorized area.
4. Email, postings on an electronic bulletin board, or in a newsgroup make references to a theft to unauthorized access or to weaknesses in the company's security system.
5. An employee reports suspicious activity by a coworker, a vendor, or a consultant.
6. An employee reports social engineering attempts on him or her.
7. An employee is approached at a technical meeting with questions from a new contact that seems suspicious.

Computer Forensics, How it can Help:

The questions technical and forensic examination can answer are:

1. When and from where the user account was accessed?
2. Are there changes in the pattern of usage on the computer?
3. Did the user understand how to navigate the system?
4. Is it possible to identify nodes and IP addresses?
5. What has been the user's previous activity on this server?

CHRONOLOGY

1585–Sir Francis Walsingham's intelligence network functioning.

1587–Christopher Marlowe's play *Tamburlaine.*

1587–Marlowe operates as a spy in the Low Countries of Europe.

1620–Francis Bacon's *Novum Organon.*

1625–Bacon's *New Atlantis.*

Eighteenth Century–British textiles, hardware, steel, coke-iron, and glass all become targets of industrial espionage. French and English manufacturers "borrow" glass technologies from each other (1773–1790).

1811–1813–Francis Cabot Lowell spies on British textile mills.

1813–Lowell, based upon his observations in Britain, hires a mechanic to build a scale model of the Cartwright loom. This step leads to building the mill complex in Lowell, Massachusetts.

1855–Allan Pinkerton combats industrial espionage against the railroads.

1860–Timothy Webster, a Pinkerton agent, guards the Perryville railroad ferry point across the Susquehanna River to protect President-elect Lincoln's train to Washington. The event foreshadows the role railroads will play in the American Civil War and the rising importance of technology in American life.

1860s–American Civil War–Aerial balloons usher in aerial reconnaissance. The Tredegar Iron Works in Richmond, Virginia becomes the arsenal for the Confederacy.

1861–Mrs. E.H. Baker's visit to Tredegar Iron Works. She sees a submarine under construction. And, she witnesses a "submarine battery" test.

1880s–John D. Rockefeller's Standard Oil engages in industrial espionage.

Late Nineteenth Century–Andrew Carnegie admits that he could not have created his steel industry in America without gathering intelligence in Europe.

1927–1938–Despite extensive physical security by American industry and the military, the Nazis steal the Norden bombsight by 1938.

1940s–The Russians, even before the bomb drops on Japan, acquire Atomic bomb secrets.

1950–The CIA holds its first meeting on the issue of economic intelligence.

1959–Edward E. Furash's article, "Industrial Espionage" in the *Harvard Business Review.*

1966–Richard Greene's book, *Business Intelligence.*

1970–Japanese begin major intelligence efforts toward the American auto industry. The President's Foreign Intelligence Advisory Board not sure what to do about the problem.

1972–Russian intelligence monitors calls about a grain purchase with the U.S.

1977–Stansfield Turner of the CIA recognizes the national security threat of industrial espionage.

1982–*Countering Industrial Espionage* book by Peter Heims.

1985–The database "Socrates" to monitor the flow of key technologies proposed by Michael Sekora at the Defense Intelligence Agency.

1990s–Russian intelligence regularly monitors American telephone traffic.

1992–*Newsweek* Article on economic espionage techniques.

1993–Factory visit at McDonnell Douglas.

1994–National Economic Council recognizes the rising threat of economic espionage.

1996–Federal Economic Espionage Act.

1997–Trade secrets cases under the Act: Gillette, Avery Dennison Corporation. (The Gillette case dealt with the alleged theft of a new shaving system. The Avery Dennison case involved a twenty-one count indictment alleging industrial spying over the period 1989-1997.)

BIBLIOGRAPHY

Archer, J.M. (1993). *Sovereignty and Intelligence: Spying and Court Culture in the English Renaissance.* Stanford, CA: Stanford University Press.

Aston, W.B., & Klavans, R.A., editors. (1997). *Keeping Abreast of Science and Technology, Technical Intelligence for Business.* Columbus, OH: Battelle Press.

Axelrod, A. (1992). *The War Between the Spies: A History of Espionage During the American Civil War.* New York: Atlantic Monthly Press.

Barry, M., & Penenberg, A. (2000). *Spooked: Espionage in Corporate America.* Cambridge, MA: Perseus Publishing.

Broder, J.F. (1984). *Risk Analysis and the Security Survey.* Newton, MA: Butterworth-Heinemann, second edition 1999.

Cartmell, D. (2001). *The Civil War Book of Lists.* Franklin Lake, NJ: New Page Books.

Catton, B. (1985). *The Civil War.* American Heritage.

Cheney, M. (1981). *Tesla, Man Out of Time.* New York: Dell Publishing.

Chernow, R. (1998). *Titan: The Life of John D. Rockefeller, Sr.* New York: Random House.

Churchill, W.S. (1974). *A History of the English-Speaking Peoples: The New World* (Volume 2). New York: Bantam.

——. (1974). *A History of the English-Speaking Peoples: The Age of Revolution* (Volume 3). New York: Bantam.

Dew, C.B. (1987). *Ironmaker to the Confederacy: Joseph R. Anderson and the Tredegar Iron Works.* Wilmington, NC: Broadfoot Publishing Co.

Dr-K. (2000). *A Complete Hacker's Handbook.* London: Carlton Books.

Fialka, J.J. (1997). *War by Other Means: Economic Espionage in America.* New York: W.W. Norton & Company.

Fischer, R.J., & Green, G. (1992). *Introduction to Security,* fifth edition. Newton, MA: Butterworth-Heinemann.

Forta, B. (2000). *SAMS Teach Yourself SQL in 10 Minutes.* SAMS Publishing.

Greene, Jr., R.M., editor. (1996). *Business Intelligence and Espionage.* New York: Dow Jones-Irwin.

Guisnel, J. (1997). *Cyberwars: Espionage on the Internet.* New York: Plenum Trade.

Harris, J.R. (1998). *Industrial Espionage and Technology Transfer: Britain and France in the 18th Century.* Brookfield, VT: Ashgate.

Heims, P. (1982). *Countering Industrial Espionage.* 20th Century Security Education Ltd., England.

Hughes-Wilson, Col. J. (1999). *Military Intelligence Blunders.* New York: Carroll & Graf.

Ive, P. (1589). *The Practice of Fortification.*

Jones, R.V. (1978). *The Wizard War.*

Kahaner, L. (1996). *Competitive Intelligence.* New York: Simon & Schuster.

Kane, H.T. (1954). *Spies for the Blue and Gray.* Garden City, NY: Hanover House.

Keegan, J. (1996). *Fields of Battle: The Wars for North America.* New York: Alfred A. Knopf.

Knightmare, T. (1994). *Secrets of a Super Hacker.* Port Townsend, WA: Loompanics Unlimited.

Koberg, D., & Bagnall, J. (1976). *The Universal Traveler.* William Kaufman.

Kobetz, R.W., editor. (1991). *Providing Executive Protection.* Executive Protection Institute.

Machiavelli, N. (1966). *The Prince* (Donno, Daniel translator). New York: Bantam Classics.

Mack, J. (1996). *Running a Ring of Spies.* Boulder, CO: Paladin Press.

Marcinko, R., & Weisman, J. (2002). *Detachment Bravo.* New York: Pocket Star Books.

Mendell, R.L. (1997). *How to Conduct Business Investigations and Competitive Intelligence Gathering.* Austin, TX: Thomas Investigative Publications.

——. (2000). How to Do Financial Asset Investigations, 2nd edition. Springfield, IL: Charles C. Thomas.

Nicholl, C. (1992). *The Reckoning: The Murder of Christopher Marlowe.* New York: Harcourt Brace & Company.

Pfaffenberger, B. (1997). *Protect Your Privacy on the Internet.* New York: John Wiley & Sons, Inc.

Porta, G. della. (1563). *De Furtivis Literarum Notis.*

Rowan, R.W. (1931). *The Pinkertons.* Boston: Little, Brown, and Company.

Russell, R., & Cunningham, S., editors. (2000). *Hack Proofing Your Network: Internet Tradecraft.* Syngress.

Schiffman, M., editor. (2001). *Hacker's Challenge.* New York: McGraw-Hill.

Schneier, B. (2000). *Secrets & Lies: Digital Security in a Networked World.* New York: John Wiley & Sons.

Schweizer, P. (1993). *Friendly Spies: How America's Allies Are Using Economic Espionage to Steal Our Secrets.* New York: Atlantic Monthly Press.

Scott, R. (1998). *The Investigator's Little Black Book 2.* Beverly Hills, CA: Crime Time Publishing Co.

Seifer, M.J. (1996). *Wizard, The Life and Times of Nikola Tesla: Biography of a Genius.* Secaucus, NJ: Birch Lane Press.

Shimomura, T. (with Markoff, J.). (1996). *Takedown.* New York: Hyperion.

Singh, S. (1999). *The Code Book.* New York: Doubleday.

Stoll, C. (1989). *The Cuckoo's Egg.* New York: Doubleday.

Sun, T. (1971). *The Art of War.* (Griffith, Samuel B., translator). London: Oxford University Press.

VanGundy, A.B. (1983). *108 Ways to Get a Bright Idea.* Upper Saddle River, NJ: Prentice Hall.

Winkler, I. (1997). *Corporate Espionage.* Rocklin, CA: Prima Publishing.

ARTICLES

Anna, C. "To Austin Startup Worker Was A Spy, Not A Moonlighter," *Austin American-Statesman,* July 15, 2002.

Bass, A. "Defense Against the Black Arts," *Darwin,* June 2001.

Denver Post, "Global Intrigue on Information Highway," April 24, 1994.

Economist, "For Pills, Not Projectiles," July 12, 1997, 344:8025.

Elias, Paul, "Prosecuting Biotech Spy Cases Proves Nettlesome," (Associated Press), *Austin American-Statesman,* August 5, 2002.

Fialka, John J., "While America Sleeps," *Wilson Quarterly,* Winter 1997, 21:1.

Friedman, Richard S., "Book Review: War by Other Means: Economic Intelligence and Industrial Espionage," *Parameters: US Army War College,* Autumn 1998, 28:3.

Furash, Edward E., "Industrial Espionage," *Harvard Business Review,* December 1959.

Mendell, Ronald L., "Ask Me No Secrets, I'll tell You No Lies," *Security Management,* May 1994, 38:5.

——, "Home Sweet Home? Protecting Sensitive Information: A Primer for Executives," *Executive Update,* September 2000.

——, "The Information Predator," *Security Management,* May 1994, 38:5.

——, "Observation Still Matters," *PI Magazine,* Spring 1996, 9:1.

Olney, Claude W., "The Secret World of the Industrial Spy," *Business and Society Review,* Winter 1988, Issue 64.

Online, May/June 2002 Issue, 26:3.

Oppel Jr., Richard A., "E-Mail Shows Enron Official Used Firm To Punish Broker Who Said 'Sell'," (*The New York Times* Service), *Austin American-Statesman,* March 27, 2002.

Seattle Times, "Software Suspect Under House Arrest," April 16, 1994.

Waller, Douglas, "The Open Barn Door: U.S. Firms Face a Wave of Foreign Espionage," *Newsweek,* May 4, 1992.

White-Collar Crime Fighter, "The Con's Latest Ploy," March 2002, 4:3.

Wylie, Margie, "Information Security Poses Serious Concern with Used Computers," *Austin American-Statesman,* June 23, 2002.

ENCYCLOPEDIA ARTICLES

"Commonplace Books," *The Encyclopedia Sherlockiana,* Jack Tracy, Avenel Books, 1977.

"Four Freedoms," *Academic American Encyclopedia,* Grolier, 1997.

MANUSCRIPTS

"Timothy Webster: Spy," William Gilmore Beymer Papers, Center for American History, The University of Texas at Austin.

SELECTED WEB SITES

"A Gentle Introduction to SQL." http://sqlzoo.net/

American Society for the Advancement of Project Management. http://www.asapm.org/

Bacon, Francis, The New Atlantis online. http://www.orst.edu/instruct/phl302/texts/bacon/atlantis.html.

Bacon, Francis, The New Organon online. http://www.constitution.org/bacon/nov_org.htm.

Bass, Alison, "Defense Against the Black Arts," *Darwin,* June 2001. http://www.darwinmag.com/read/060101/defense.html

Brenner, Susan, "The Development of Private Policing," University of Dayton School of Law. http://cybercrimes.net/Private/early.html

Computer Forensics and Evidence. http://www.computer-data-forensics-evidence-discovery.com/.

"Cryptography," (Copyright © Francis Litterio). http://world.std.com/~franl/crypto.html.

Dean, Joshua, "Lost Laptops Compromise Secrets." http://www.govexec.com/features/1001/1001managetech2.htm.

DIALOG. http://www.dialog.com

Economic Espionage Act of 1996. http://execpc.com/~mhallign/federal.html

EDGAR. http://www.sec.gov/edgar.shtml

Elias, Stephen, "Trade Secret Law: Overview." http://www.marketingtoday.com/legal/tradesec.htm/.

Ellison, Craig, "Yes, Wireless LANS Are Vulnerable, But Yours Doesn't Have To Be." http://www.extremetech.com/article2/0,3973,11388,00.asp.

The Fair Credit Reporting Act. http://www.ftc.gov/os/statutes/fcra.htm.

LexisNexis. http://www.lexisnexis.com

Mendell, Ronald L., "Vulnerable Databases: Sleuthing with AWK and SQL." http://www.info-sec.com/internet/01/internet_082101a_j.shtml.

Mendell, Ronald L., "Home Sweet Home? Protection Sensitive Information: A Primer for Executives." http://www.gwsae.org/ExecutiveUpdate/2000/September/HomeSweet.htm.

National Air and Space Museum, "The Spy Skies." http://www.nasm.edu/galleries/lae/html/sky_early.htm.

Privacy Violations by an Employer. http:www.divorcelawinfo2.com/mylawyer/.

Ryan, Joe, "Competitive Intelligence Sources on the Internet." http://web.syr.edu/~jryan/infopro/intell.html.

Security Management magazine. http://www.securitymanagement.com.

Society of Competitive Intelligence Professionals (SCIP) http://www.scip.org

Thornton, Anthony, "End-of-Life Data Security in the Enterprise." http://www.redemtech.com/extaudit//news_research/ds_whitepaper.pdf.

INDEX